North and West
Scotland

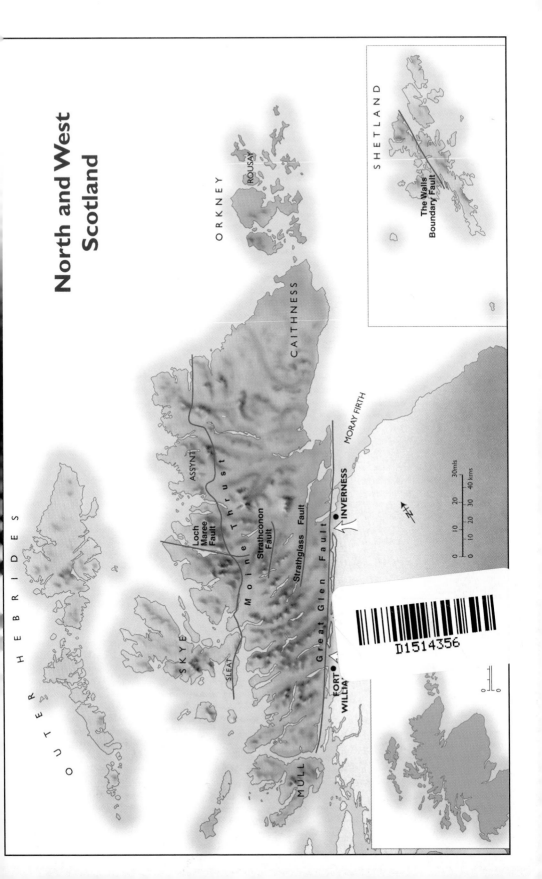

OUTER HEBRIDES

SKYE

SLEAT

MULL

ASSYNT

Loch Maree Fault

Moine Thrust

Strathconon Fault

Strathglass Fault

Great Glen Fault

FORT WILLIAM

INVERNESS

MORAY FIRTH

CAITHNESS

ORKNEY

ROUSAY

SHETLAND

The Walls Boundary Fault

N

| 0 | 10 | 20 | 30mls |
| 0 | 10 | 20 | 30 | 40 kms |

Strathglass is a fault-guided valley, parallel to the Great Glen. Deepened by glacial action, its floor has since filled with alluvial sediments, through which the river has wound an intricate pattern of channels. The mainly birch wood (left) represents regrowth after a cutting of the original woodland, while the tall, exotic conifers to the right are Victorian amenity planting

Loch Broom, a sea-loch near Ullapool, with birch woodland growing only where protected from grazing

Robin Noble has inhabited and studied the landscape of Assynt for over 30 years. A former graduate of Cambridge, he ran the Orkney Field Centre, then the Aigas Field Centre, near Beauly. He has lectured at Glasgow Caledonian and Stirling Universities, and is highly regarded as an environmental expert.

'This book is a companion, to be taken with you in your rucksack and dipped into as you munch your sandwiches under a gnarled old pine, or stand mesmerised by the play of light and shadow on the surface of a loch far below. I commend it to everyone ...'

SIR JOHN LISTER-KAYE,
FORMER PRESIDENT OF THE SCOTTISH WILDLIFE TRUST

'Robin Noble writes with passion, broad insight and tremendous commitment ... compelling to anyone with the least pride and ambition in the potential of Scotland's nature and people.'

SIMON PEPPER,
DIRECTOR OF WWF, SCOTLAND

NORTH AND WEST

First published 2003 by

SCOTTISH CULTURAL PRESS

Unit 6, Newbattle Abbey Business Park
Newbattle Road, DALKEITH EH22 3LJ Scotland
Tel: +44 (0)131 660 6366 • Fax: +44 (0)131 660 4666
Email: info@scottishbooks.com
www.scottishbooks.com

'Envoi' by Robert Rendall is reproduced on page 115
by kind permission of his nephew, Robert P. Rendall

COVER IMAGES: Quinag from near Oldany, Assynt *(top)*; Loch
Eishort from near Ord, Sleat *(bottom)*. Map on back cover and at
beginning of book copyright © Wendy Price Cartographic Services

BRITISH LIBRARY CATALOGUING IN PUBLICATION DATA
A catalogue record for this book is available from the British Library

ISBN: 1 84017 029 8

Print and bound by Bell & Bain Ltd, Glasgow

North and West

Exploring the
North and **West**
Highlands and Islands of Scotland

Robin Noble

SCOTTISH CULTURAL PRESS

In Memoriam

Joyce Isabel Menzies (née Munro)

1896–1994

my grandmother, whose wide knowledge and deep love of
the Scottish Highlands and Islands helped to form my own

Contents

Foreword

JOHN LISTER-KAYE

Once in a while, in my experience very rarely, one comes across a person or a book, or a work of art, whose quality of distinction is immediately apparent and without the exercise of critical faculty. I think this little book and its author are one of these.

Of course, I have the advantage of knowing the subject, that area of the Highlands wrapped in mountains and mists, and dark and complicated history, where I have chosen to live and work for the past thirty years. And I know its writer – have had the privilege and delight of working alongside him – through long, dreich winters and high radiant days in the hills, good times and bad, for more of those years than I now care to count!

So my view is subjective; but so is this little book. That is an important part of its charm. Robin Noble takes you with him as an equal and a companion, back through the first impressions of his childhood adventures in Assynt, back to the very violent volcanic beginnings of the landscape itself, explaining, enquiring, exploring and observing. Sometimes he is just chatting to you from the depths of his remarkable knowledge and experience, sometimes offering a serious treatise on archaeology or wildlife, until finally and inevitably he is justifying the world of change in which we are all caught up, and its visible impact on that most precious human resource, the very wildness of the place and the very personal spiritual rejuvenation one discovers afresh every time one steps out into the Rough Bounds.

This book is not a guide, but it is a companion, in the true sense of the word, to be taken with you in your rucksack and dipped into as you, like the writer, munch your sandwiches under a gnarled old pine, or stand mesmerised by the play of light and shadow on the surface of a loch far below. I commend it to everyone in whom, like me, the Highlands evokes a strange and wonderful world in which all our emotions find intenser reflections. Perhaps it is the lost world of childhood, of the individual or the race – vision undimmed, sense of wonder unconfined.

John Lister-Kaye
House of Aigas

A past President of the Scottish Wildlife Trust, Sir John Lister-Kaye is a well-known Highland conservationist and writer who has served many public bodies in the world of nature conservation, environmental education and the countryside. He is the founder director of Aigas Field Centre near Glen Affric which has been his home and his work since 1970.

Introduction

Many first-time visitors to the Scottish Highlands reach Fort William and then follow Lochs Linnhe, Lochy, Oich and Ness to Inverness. For them, the line of the Great Glen, with its main road, is an artery of communication, and as they drive north-east to Inverness, they may be vaguely aware that there is a great deal of territory off on their left. They will have heard of some of it – like the Isle of Skye – but all too often they will not have time to explore further, and will reach Inverness only to turn south. That is indeed a shame.

Although the Great Glen is in some ways an obvious line of communication, it is in a geographical sense a barrier, a defining limit. It would only require a relatively slight change in sea level for it to fill with water, and become a real obstacle. As it is, the list of lochs above makes it clear that much of its deep trench is occupied by water – if you were to walk westwards, across country from Aberdeen, avoiding bridges or ferries, you would have to make for one of only four slight land connections, and even then you would have a significant river to cross. But it would be well worth it.

The truth is that when, travelling from south or east, you reach that line and cross it, the best is before you. The land you are entering is more complicated, more spectacular, has more diversity, more interest, more problems, and far more beauty than that through which you have passed to enter it.

This book is about that land and its people. It sets out to explain some of that diversity of interest, to explore some of the charms of the North and West. Deliberately, it leaves the reader to follow up these lines of interest, to explore further, to find out things for themselves. It aims to provide an introduction, and an overall context, in which this further exploration may be seen.

The idea of this project really started when I was researching in Glencalvie, and I am grateful to Peter Fowler for his encouragement at that time, and for his permission to quote from the material gathered then. Others have given me real encouragement and advice when I needed it – notably Alastair and Sheena Scott, David Sexton, and John and Lucy Lister-Kaye. I have benefited also from discussion with Billy and Jean Munro, Barbara Crawford and Chris Smout. Jim and Margaret Payne, Ardvar, have been most co-operative. I am, of course, enormously grateful to everyone at Scottish Cultural Press for their enthusiasm for this book.

For many years I have led groups on field trips of one sort or another throughout the Highlands and Islands, and have made many friends in so doing – it is also fair to say that their constant questioning led me to decide that there was a need for a book like this!

But it is the subject of the book that has really kept me going throughout, the wonderful land of the North and West in which I have lived for 30 years, and its people whose humour, steadfastness and endless cups of coffee have made me forget the occasional rain, midge or tick!

Robin Noble
Glenleraig, Assynt

Safety in the Great Outdoors

Please note that the fact that I may have walked any particular route does not imply that it is safe or even intelligent to do so. Nor should the fact that I visited any particular site be taken as an indication that the site itself is safe or, indeed, open to the public. Venturing off the road in the north-west Highlands and Islands is a serious decision to make, for which the responsibility can only be yours. It can bring great rewards, of course, but you must ensure that you are properly prepared.

Do carry ~

      spare clothing
      food and drink
      a torch
      First Aid kit
      whistle
      emergency survival bag

This sounds heavy, but with modern fabrics, etc, it need not be, and all are available quite cheaply at specialist climbing/walking/camping stores in most large towns.

Don't forget your map and compass, and please make sure you know how to use them!

Do wear properly designed footwear, with good gripping soles and real ankle support; and have spare laces with you.

Do try to learn to walk with a stick or, if you must be high-tech, one or two walking poles! These really are among the most important safety aids that exist, as loss of balance is one of the most common causes of outdoor accidents – when did you last hear of a shepherd who broke a leg out on the hill?

It is always advisable to walk in a group. Make sure you leave a route plan with someone who will be expecting your return, together with your mobile phone number, if you have one.

Equally important, I think, is the attitude with which you set off – be prepared and organised in your approach to a long day out. Check the predicted weather forecasts and assess whether it is safe to embark. Note the time that you leave the road, work out when you should turn or reach a certain point. Be humble, leave the countryside as you found it and would like to find it: for instance, quite empty of litter! Respect other people's use and enjoyment of the countryside, too.

Above all, keep calm whatever happens – nothing, not even thick mist can make you jump over a cliff if you don't want to! Do be reasonable, don't go out in foul weather; it's uncomfortable, you won't see a thing, and if it gets much worse it could kill you, even in Scotland.

Know your limits – remember when 'conquering' a mountain, or 'bagging' another summit that they can just as easily 'bag' you. It is unlikely that humility will kill you, but over-confidence certainly can. Be willing to learn from the countryside and from your own reactions to it.

And enjoy it!

1: *The Walk to Ardvar*

JULY 1961

For much of my youth, my mind was dominated by one mountain – Quinag. I had known it for many years before I actually set foot on it – part of the remarkable outline of its ridge could be seen clearly from the skylight window of the attic bedroom in the holiday cottage where we spent as much of each year as possible.

At that time we lived, officially and regrettably as far as I was concerned, in Fife and I went to school in Perthshire. There, in the summer term, we were encouraged to explore the freedom of the hills on the Highlands' southern edge. I enjoyed the independence, but found the hills disappointing – like large puddings, rounded and dull for the most part. It was there that I realised that I was by now accustomed to a mountain background of greater grandeur, which I had so far neglected. I resolved that the coming summer would see me exploring these more impressive hills – and so it did.

Since 1959, we had spent the long summer holidays, and at times also part of the Easter, in Assynt, an area that was then considered remote. The journey from Fife was certainly epic, by the old, caravan-clogged A9 as far north as Bonar Bridge, and from there by single-track road westwards. Going up the Oykell, there was a moment when we could see the single peak of Canisp, and then, once on Craggie, the remarkable shapes of Cul Mor and Suilven – we were getting there. Once Quinag was sighted, our spirits soared, for our destination lay in the shadow of that mountain. The peaks of its long western ridge were the ones that we could see from our bedroom skylight and the burn that murmured us to sleep – or, at times, roared in the wild night – flowed from its mighty cliffs.

Our cottage lay in its deep wooded glen, but the easiest way up the mountain was to follow the road out of the glen and over the foothills towards the long slope – An Leathad Leireag – which led up to the great western cliffs. Despite their forbidding aspect, there was, and is, an easy enough line of ascent from here. It was, however, steep and involved the negotiation of a boulder-field resting on sand, at times unpleasantly mobile. We heaved ourselves up this section to the point where a small, abrupt, square outcrop of cliff seemed to mark a transition to an easier gradient. Here we stopped to draw breath and to admire the view. It was indeed glorious.

At our feet were two lochs, one large and deep-set, with a wooded corrie at its back. From there, the deepening trench of our glen ran to the north-west, at first through an apparent emptiness of deergrass and rock, then increasingly through birch woodlands to the sea. To the west of the glen was the wonderful, crazy puzzle of rock and water that is the map of Assynt, terminating in the cleancut shape of the Point of Stoer, and the bright waters of the Minch. Somewhat to the east of all this, and almost at our feet, smoother, sloping land led the eye down to another loch, apparently land-locked but, in fact, an arm of the sea. Beyond the rough headlands which enclosed it, was a magical backdrop of islands and, perfectly placed beside the waters of the loch, was one white house. This was Ardvar.

Ardvar was an old lodge, and remarkable – even in 1959 – in that it had neither telephone nor electricity and could not be reached by car; one either walked or went by boat. We had made a number of sorties there, but one stands out in my memory.

I can still see the group of us walking the narrow path from the twisting single-track road. There were quite a number of us, including a few youngsters like my brother and myself, clad in jeans and wellies. We carried game-bags over our shoulders, containing the boxes of sandwiches intended for lunch; though, at least to my mind, they were not in the end the highlight of the day. (They were made of corned beef, which I detested and, having been kept in the local shop's deep freeze overnight, were half-frozen, even when we came to eat them.) Around us were women, many of them black-skirted, and older men, mostly clad in elderly plus-fours or equally aged overalls. There were dogs – collies, of course – everywhere, the unreliable untrained younger dogs leaping and barking around us, while the older animals were allowed to run free on the hill for the day.

Our path ran along a steep heather slope with scattered birches and rowans. Below us were the blue waters of the sea loch, edged now at low tide by that striking line of white rock above black, itself above a fringe of orange and ochre seaweed. The head of the loch was shallow and, just where it got deeper, there was a small green islet on which lay the tumbled, grey walls of a ruined circular prehistoric fort. The map called it a 'broch'. Whenever I asked anyone what a broch was, they said it was a Pictish tower, but did not elaborate. The coursed walling of the interior was quite clear, with a great deal of debris masking the outer face, so that it looked as if it had somehow all been pushed outwards.

Further along, our track crossed a burn and then zigzagged over a low green hill, from where it could be seen that we were approaching the whitewashed house, and close by it, the sheds and 'fank' or sheepfold. We would have known where to head in any case, because of the noise made by the sheep which had been gathered earlier.

Soon the scene was, at least to our inexperienced eyes, wonderfully chaotic. The sheep had been gathered for the clipping, but the lambs had to be separated first of all from their mothers and the air was loud with their lamentations and the barking of the excited dogs. The fank was old and somewhat makeshift, and every now and then a determined ewe took a flying leap over a fence or a wall and erupted into our midst. One did so and promptly died on landing, presumably from heart failure. It was left lying in a corner while everyone got on with the business of the day and to our macabre fascination it soon began to swell.

Once the sorting was over, the clipping began in earnest and some sort of production-line was set up. A couple of the men were responsible for catching sheep and trundling them over to the clippers. Each man flipped the sheep over on its back, held it between his knees and rapidly and expertly clipped away the thick fleece. We boys stood by with a pot of what looked like engine-oil (which we dabbed on any cuts or nicks the sheep might experience during the process) and with tins of sticky red 'buist' or marking-fluid. The paint dripped very effectively and we were soon sticky with it, and sweating furiously as we darted to and fro to mark each newly-clipped sheep with 'A' for Ardvar. The background to all this work was a constant stream of laughter and joking. My brother got carried away to the extent that he was soon threatening to 'buist' one of his tormentors – a small, lively, middle-aged lady called Molly.

When we stopped for lunch the icy sandwiches were produced and washed down – tea for us, and some whisky or beer for the more fortunate. This only helped to quicken the pace and the hilarity in the afternoon. Then, perhaps to ensure that we were not totally covered in buist, we were sent to assist with the rolling of the fleeces. This was done on a door laid over trestles and our hands soon acquired a layer of oil from the wool – we were told it was good for the skin. Then we carried the rolled-up fleeces into a shed where a huge sack had been suspended from the rafters. One young man had the unenviable job of standing in the woolsack, catching the fleeces we threw up to him and treading them down under his feet. It was a warm day and one could hardly imagine a sweatier occupation. There did indeed come from one of the bolder ladies the suggestion that he should strip for the task, the wool being so good for the skin. But the lad, who was already red enough in the face, merely went one shade deeper and dived back into his sack!

Eventually, the work of the day was done and we gathered up

our possessions and walked back to the vehicles. In the west, the sinking sun sent a golden glow over our long strung-out party as it wended its way along the rocky track. The talk was quieter now, contented after a day's activity, and much of it was in Gaelic which neither my brother nor I could understand. I was happy to look at the faces of our friends, lined, weather-beaten, friendly and kind, and to listen to the lilt of their voices.

The one thing, of course, you do not realise at the age of eleven is that you are taking part in a way-of-life that is soon to disappear for ever. That summer we also helped with peat-stacking, and harvesting oats and hay, all being cut and put up by hand. Apart from the glory of that long, long-ago summer, I still remember the joy of helping with a necessary task, of achieving something for and with people who clearly belonged. They, and that, mattered to me. It still does.

This book is about the North and West of Scotland, its land and people, its past and present, perhaps even its future.

2: *The Bones of the Land*

THE NATURE AND SHAPING OF THE HIGHLAND COUNTRYSIDE

Many years later I stood on the summit of a remote hill in central Ross-shire, looking all around. It was a very hot day and, scantily clad as I was, I was dripping with the effort of the climb. My view seemed to take in the greater part of North and West Scotland but my eyes were, inevitably, drawn first to the west, for there, sharply etched on the horizon, were the remarkable shapes of the hills of my youth, from Ben More Coigach to Quinag. Their abrupt outlines contrasted with the grey-backed, sprawling masses of Conival, Ben More Assynt and Ben Hee.

Due north was the strange profile of Loyal and then the canted shape of Clibreck, while to the east, still wreathed in the tendrils of morning mist, were the Griams and the unexpected hills of Caithness. The eastern plain was quite hidden in the haar, except for one startling glimpse of the Cromarty Firth. There, over a vignette of level green fields, loomed the incongruous outline of an oil rig.

From this vantage point, I was in fact seeing the full breadth of Northern Scotland, from west to east; a panorama which clearly presents a geological sequence. Roughly speaking, the older rocks are to the west, the younger to the east.

In the west, the dramatic mountains of Assynt rest on a basement of ancient rock called Lewisian Gneiss. There it appears on the surface (as it does in Lewis – from where it takes its name –

and, indeed, throughout the Outer Hebrides), but it is elsewhere often covered by younger rocks. The gneiss is incredibly old, being a fragment of the ancient continental crust, up to 3,000 million years in age. When it formed, the world was still unstable and the processes to which the rock was subjected have led to its original nature being completely altered or metamorphosed: the word 'metamorphic' is applied to this sort of rock. In effect, as the earth's crust cooled, it was like a thick soup, forming a skin which wrinkled – but of course on a gigantic scale.

Some areas of rock show signs of having been carried down below the surface (into the wrinkles!) towards the molten core, to a depth as great as 50 kilometres, where they were subjected to great heat and partially re-melted, before being uplifted and again cooled. This may have happened repeatedly over a long period, and the rock so formed is hard, rough and markedly irregular in structure, not to say contorted. As in Assynt and the Outer Hebrides where the seams and wrinkles in its ancient fabric are occupied by the water of burns or lochs, it can present a geography of remarkable complexity – the crazy puzzle of rock and water over which we looked from Quinag.

The Lewisian landscape of Assynt had been eroded down to its present level by about 1,000 million years ago, around which time sediment from a neighbouring land mass began to be deposited right across the gneiss of what is now Northern Scotland. In Assynt and Coigach and other west-coast areas, this deposit, the Torridonian Sandstone, appears virtually undisturbed in its horizontal bedding, easily visible in the cliffs of mountains such as Suilven and Quinag, and perhaps most magnificently in the Torridon hills which, of course, lend it its name. This rock gives the mountains their characteristically steep, well-cliffed sides and purplish colour. It is resistant to erosion, but eventually breaks down to form a coarse sand often to be found in the gullies of these hills – this can make climbing exciting!

The summits of these mountains may be flat and pavement-like, or a series of pinnacles and towers exemplified perhaps by the ridge of Stac Pollaidh in Wester Ross. At a lower level, the massive expanses of this sandstone present an effective barrier to the drainage of surface water, and so are often covered by waterlogged moor.

These hills are so impressive and solid in appearance that it is hard to remember that these substantial mountains are just the eroded remnants of immense sheets of deposit, and that those sheets themselves were subject to vertical movement and tilting through subsequent millions of years. Looking at the stratification (layers of rock) on the southern face of Canisp, it can be seen that the Torridonian must have tilted and sunk before a rock of marine origin was laid down in its own horizontal beds at a higher level. When the sandstone was subsequently uplifted, it resumed its horizontal bedding, leaving the bands of the higher rock to form a long dip-slope to the east. This rock is now the hard, splintery rock called Cambrian Quartzite that protects the summits of so many sandstone mountains. Its long, grey dip-slopes provide an easy angle of access to Spidean Coinnich of Quinag, to Canisp and other hills. This quartzite is also our first rock to show proof of animal life in the seas of the age: there are wormcasts visible in what is called 'piperock'.

Between these west-coast areas and the central tracts of the Northern Highlands, there exists a frontier which is clearly visible on geological maps – the line of the Moine Thrust. It is a boundary of great significance, marking the westward limit of the upheaval caused by one or more periods of mountain building. The Moine rocks to the east of this line are sedimentary in origin like the sandstone to the west, but they were metamorphosed in the contorting process of mountain building. The line of the Moine Thrust marks where the mobile mass to the east came up against the stable foreland of the west; in that process, the older rocks of the basement were pushed up over the younger in a very complex fashion. This is well seen in Assynt and is particularly visible from the road at Loch Glencoul.

The sediments to the east of this line are probably related to the Torridonian, and there is evidence that they were laid down in shallow water conditions. Relatively unaltered areas show signs of being mud and sand deposits, with rain-pittings, sun-cracks and ripple-marks. The Caledonian and earlier orogenies (periods of mountain-building) subjected the sediments of these Moine Rocks to intense deformation and re-crystallisation. Mountain-building is thought of simply as 'folding', but the complexity of the process in the Northern Highlands may be gauged by the fact that in some places slices of the Lewisian basement have been scooped up and refolded or interleaved with Moine rocks. The resultant rock is hard and gives rise to the sort of scenery which is perceived as 'typically Highland'. Much of the central spine of the Highlands is indeed composed of this rock.

Impressive as is the scenery produced by these rocks – for instance in the Affric Hills – those that remain are insignificant compared to the mountains which were the immediate result of the Caledonian orogeny. They may have been on the scale of the Alps or even of the Himalayas, and wide rivers flowing east from them carried great quantities of sediment on to alluvial flats around the present Moray Firth. These consolidated sediments eventually formed the rock we know as the Old Red Sandstone, which appears to the east of the Northern Highlands, in the fertile lands of East Sutherland, Easter Ross and the Black Isle. Related sedimentary rocks cover large areas of Caithness and virtually all of Orkney. This rock is much softer than that of the metamorphosed Highland area and more porous, giving rise to the smooth landforms and well-draining soils of the east.

As seen in these areas, the nature of the rock in any one area, and the formations in which it appears, are of considerable importance in determining the soils and the natural vegetation of that location. This can be seen to a remarkable degree just to the west of the Moine Thrust, where a band of limestone of Cambrian age and younger appears at Durness, Inchnadamph-Stronchrubie and Elphin-Knockan in Assynt; Kishorn in Wester Ross; between Broadford and Torrin in Skye; and also at Ord in Sleat. This limestone is fairly porous and free-draining, and gives rise to a short, sweet turf, with some specialist flowers, notably the dryas octopetala or mountain avens. These green areas differ visibly from their immediate surroundings (despite experiencing the same extremes of climate) where, on largely impermeable rock, bog and wet moorland predominate. The limestone areas are also remarkable for their extensive cave systems, potholes and underground rivers.

Limestone also makes a significant difference to the landscape of Shetland where it appears in the green valley of Tingwall. Shetland itself is geologically most complex, being a detached microcosm of the Northern Highlands and containing within its relatively small area rocks of all periods so far referred to, as well as younger sediments and volcanic rocks.

The erosion of millions of years stripped away much of the covering of younger sedimentary rocks, but they still remain in some places. Fossil beds may be found in such areas, as in Skye between Ashaig (near Broadford) and Suishnish; at Eathie on the Black Isle; Balintore in Easter Ross; from Golspie to Helmsdale in East Sutherland and elsewhere.

During the passage of the millions of years outlined above, there have been many episodes of volcanic activity. Several of the masses of igneous rock produced in these episodes have been themselves subject to subsequent folding and at least partial metamorphism, which can make them, to the casual observer, indistinguishable from the bulk of the Moine rocks. That is certainly not the case with the youngest volcanic rocks which cover a significant part of this area.

Approximately 60 million years ago, there was considerable volcanic activity centred on Arran, Mull, Ardnamurchan, Rum and the Skye Cuillin. From these centres there poured out sheets of lava which now form, for instance, the bulk of the Isle of Skye north of the Cuillins, as well as much of Mull and Morvern. These sheets of lava produce a very distinctive landscape – plateaux with steep escarpments – whose cliffs may be merely roughly columnar in form or show the splendid regularity of basalt, as at the famous Fingal's Cave in Staffa, the Shiant Islands or the lesser-known hills of Skye, Preshal Mor and Preshal Beag. These lava plateaux are somewhat better draining than the metamorphic rocks and produce a rather more fertile soil, although this is partly offset by the fact that the level surfaces of the plateaux themselves are prone to waterlogging and the formation of peat.

The Black and Red Cuillin of Skye are both volcanic in origin, representing igneous rocks that have formed under different conditions. The Black Cuillin are not so much the visible remains of the volcano, but of the chamber under the volcanic cone. The rock from which they are formed is called 'gabbro' and is remarkably tough. It has created the most dramatic, not to say savage, mountains in the British Isles, beloved of climbers.

The spectacular events which produced the great lava flows ripped cracks – both vertical and horizontal – in the surrounding landscapes, through which there flowed molten rock; the vertical cracks are called 'dykes' and the horizontal are called 'sills'. Because the dykes are vertical cracks, they may be very vulnerable to erosion; often the cooled igneous rock may be harder than the shattered matrix rock and remain upstanding, like a wall. Swarms of these dykes centre on the old volcanoes and are a very prominent feature of the geology of Mull and Skye in particular. The walker, for instance at the very southern tip of Sleat, may find his or her way barred by deep, vertical-sided trenches where the upwelling molten rock has proved significantly softer than that which surrounded it.

There have, of course, always been such weaknesses in rock, and the old Lewisian basement itself shows many such dykes. Other areas of weakness occur where bodies of rock have moved past each other, resulting in the crushing and fragmentation of material on both sides. Such lines of weakness are often followed by burns and rivers.

The deeply incised rivers which carried the sediment from the mountains to the Moray Firth Basin seem to have flowed roughly from west to east. One such river must have used the line now represented by Glen Cannich and Glen Urquhart. But this original (technically, the 'consequent') drainage pattern has been remarkably disrupted by a series of major, parallel faults – the Great Glen, Strath Glass and Strath Conon faults – whose straight lines are so conspicuous on our maps. These intersect the consequent valley pattern at an acute angle.

These faults and others seem to have been already in existence before the deposition of the Old Red Sandstone, and the Great Glen fault at least may have formed a major valley at that time. The effects of these faults in distorting the consequent drainage pattern are most marked. The Strath Glass fault, for instance, has disrupted the Cannich–Urquhart river, diverting the waters of the present Cannich and Affric rivers to join those of the Farrar. In a much more dramatic way, the Great Glen itself halts any further easterly flow of the Urquhart, diverting its water in a north-easterly direction. The Strath Glass fault is seen extending as a minor valley running north from Erchless Castle towards the Orrin, while the remarkably straight coastline of the Black Isle and its northerly prolongation to Tarbat Ness represents the northern section of the Great Glen fault. A third and parallel fault in Strath Conon may have severed the Orrin from its headwaters if it originally flowed along the Scardroy-Inverchoran line. Water from here now flows north-east along the fault to join the easterly aligned Milton–Scatwell valley.

A fault is a fracture in a rock-body, and these faults are tear-faults. The dictionary definition is 'a fault, usually steeply inclined, and along which movement (of the now divided rock masses) has been horizontal'. Because of its scale, the Great Glen Fault has attracted a great deal of study, but it is still, apparently, not yet possible to say firmly in which direction that movement has been, or over what distance! There is a real possibility that movement has been to and fro over a long period. Yet another line of faults forms the western boundary of the sandstone basin of the Moray Firth. Fault lines are visible all over the Highlands and Islands, particularly along Loch Maree, and also in Shetland.

For millions of years thereafter, the whole area was subject to erosion, both aerial and by the action of water. The next dramatic events to leave their mark were the series of extremely cold periods which have, rather misleadingly, been called the 'Ice Age', as if there were only one. They were comparatively recent, as they have occupied merely the last couple of million years. During this time, the climate fluctuated considerably, and the ice duly advanced and retreated. The principal effect of the scouring action of the heavy ice sheet was to remove material from the areas of higher land and to erode along existing lines of weakness. This resulted in the over-deepening of the fault-guided valley floors. The action of the ice was responsible for the formation of many of the deep basins occupied by lochs like Loch Affric and it gouged out the basin of Loch Ness to the great depth of over 250 metres. The full extent of this latter basin will be better understood when it is realised that it continues out from Loch Ness into the Moray Firth, a borehole sunk near Inverness having passed through about 100 metres of superficial deposits without reaching bedrock.

'Glaciation' of course is an over-simplification of a series of complicated, related events. At one stage, the whole of Scotland, probably to the highest summits, was covered by an ice sheet. Over thousands of years this sheet advanced and retreated, the later advances being limited to the formation of small valley glaciers in the higher hills. Glaciation causes both erosion and deposition, and the advancing and retreating ice left a complexity of formations that is not always easy to unravel.

The naturally gentle relief of the softer sandstone areas was further subdued by the action of ice moving eastwards from the mountains of Ross and Sutherland. This ice was sufficient in volume to deflect to the east that ice which was moving north-east along the trend of the Strath Glass and Great Glen faults. The direction of the flow of the ice has been ascertained by mapping 'erratics', boulders which conspicuously did not originate where they are now found, but can be traced to a common source. These erratics were carried, along with the ground-up material abraded from the rocks (known as 'till'), and deposited on the lower land.

The features which most immediately reflect the glaciation of this area are in reality secondary features, etched into or deposited on to the landscape which had been subjected to the overall action of the ice sheet. In the higher places, they are often the product of the small valley-glaciers, and include the classic U-shaped glaciated valley, sometimes with a V-shaped notch at its base, eroded by the subsequent action of a stream. This may be seen in many places but Gleann Chorainn, a subsidiary of Strath Conon, provides a good example. The valleys often show the small, generally rounded hummocks of 'moraines': eroded material left behind by retreating glaciers. These may be seen perhaps at their most spectacular in Glen Torridon. Other typical features are the 'corries', rounded basins in the hills often on the north-east facing slopes. These are unanimously agreed to be glacial features, although the processes which led to their formation are not completely understood. Where a number of corries do form, the peak between them will often be pyramidal in shape. The ridges between the corries are often narrow and are termed 'arêtes'. Examples of these formations are easily seen in any mountain area, in the mountains around Loch Affric, in Quinag and, magnificently, in the Black Cuillin.

The lower-lying areas show excellent examples of forms created by the arrest, decay and retreat of the ice. These include 'eskers', long sinuous moraines of which there is a particularly good example near Dornoch. There are also 'kames', rounded morainic hills associated with the margins of wasting ice, and 'kettleholes', which are depressions in glacial drift formed by the melting of a body of ice which had been buried in the drift. From Inverness, via Beauly to Muir of Ord and Garve, all these features occur and deserve examination. With them, too, are raised beaches; the A862 Inverness–Beauly road passes along the base of a raised shoreline just as it leaves Inverness. In fact, there is a whole series of shorelines associated with changes in sea level.

While the world's seas must have risen as glaciers melted, and have fallen as they re-advanced, the land itself is assumed to have sunk when depressed by the great weight of the ice sheet, and correspondingly to have risen as the ice melted. The various shorelines discernible all around the coast should be seen in this shifting context, but it is quite clear that large areas of land were formerly covered by the sea which, for instance, once extended as far inland as Fort Augustus and Contin. While the bulk of this area is still rising relative to the sea, that is not true of the Outer

Hebrides or of Orkney and Shetland, where the beach-levels are not now to be seen. These are drowned landscapes, but that does not mean that evidence for the deposition of eroded material cannot be seen around their coasts. On the contrary; material eroded from their far headlands may often be seen deposited in the form of bars or storm-beaches ('ayres' in Orkney) that impound many freshwater lochs or tidal lagoons ('oyces'). These are likely to be very recent in formation and there is evidence that islands like Sanday in Orkney have changed their shapes markedly in the last few hundred years.

Throughout the whole area, the only thing that has been constant over the last 3,000 million years has been change. Nature is not static, particularly in the Highlands and Islands, which possess, for their small area, a remarkable diversity of geology and structure. These are the very bones of the land, and understanding the land has to start here.

3: Assynt

QUINAG

As ever, I paused above the square outcrop of rock at the northern end of Quinag to look towards Ardvar and the islands of Eddrachillis, as much to draw breath as to admire the view, which was, in fact, rather misty. When I resumed, I kept more to the Kylesku side of Sail Gorm, the prominent northern peak, and as I plodded on was rewarded with a glimpse of the exciting concrete sweep of the new bridge over the narrows – the Caolas Cumhang – which has replaced the ferry of my youth. Though it is a beautiful bridge, there can be no doubt that something of the romance of the crossing has gone – but so, too, has an enormous amount of summertime frustration, as long queues used to build up. Now, despite the fact that this was the last week of July, there was little of summertime in the temperature and a really cold wind blew at this altitude. I was glad of a thick jersey and tended to keep moving.

Therefore, I did not stop long on reaching the summit of Sail Gorm, which was a shame because the view, though familiar to me, is wonderful. Quinag is a complicated mountain on something of a Y plan, with deep corries to the east and fine ridges with a variety of peaks, and they are all seen to advantage from Sail Gorm. I remembered the smooth ridge that leads from the summit as being soft and mossy; surely, on occasion, I had even taken off my boots and gone barefoot here? Now, it seemed much stonier than I recalled and I wondered if this might be the result of erosion,

A Hydro-electric reservoir is beautified by its background of mountain and Caledonian Pine Forest. This lovely woodland, with its characteristic round-topped, red-barked trees, is home to a specialised wildlife which includes the crossbill, crested-tit and capercaillie

The western cliffs of Quinag in Assynt are formed of hard, purplish Torridonian Sandstone and tower above the complex Lewisian Gneiss landscape of the plateau between the mountains and the broad channel of the Minch

caused by the greater number of folk on the hills nowadays. There was certainly a considerable number, in different parties, beginning to be visible on the hill. At the end of the day I calculated that I had easily seen three times as many as one would have expected twenty years before, especially considering the coldness. Off the obvious route along the ridges used by such parties the moss and short turf seemed much as ever, and very attractive with the soft mauve of the thyme and the yellow-green of alpine lady's mantle. I had stopped at the point on Sail Gorm where we had often seen, or heard, ptarmigan, but none were forthcoming.

The ridge from Sail Gorm narrows, giving splendid views down the gullies along the western cliffs, before one comes to an abrupt, castellated peak, whose west face shows well the horizontal bedding of the dark sandstone. After this there is a steep descent to a sandy col, before another ascent to the roughly pyramidal central peak from which the three ridges radiate. I managed to find a place at the back of this peak where the wind did not penetrate and sat down to have my lunch, watching the parties of walkers heave themselves up the side of the main summit ridge. The views to the aptly named Glasven – the grey hill – and to the twin summits of Conival and Ben More Assynt were somewhat obscured by mist, but the ranked peaks of Canisp, Suilven and the Coigach Hills were now beautifully clear.

After my sandwiches and warming coffee I walked along the narrowing ridge to the highest point – there is remarkably obvious colour change here as one moves from the purple Torridonian boulders to the sharper, grey-white quartzite which forms the principal summit. I continued past the trig. point, descending to the almost perfect pavement of sandstone slabs, which stretches ahead in a slight curve. It suddenly stops, as if cut away with a knife. When we were young we always used to stop just before the end, put down our rucksacks and other clobber, and advance slowly and cautiously to the brink. One such time we crouched down on our knees to look over and it was just as well we were not standing or I think that we would have gone over in our excitement. A golden eagle must have been on a ledge immediately below us and, as we put our heads over the edge, she launched herself into space, giving us a marvellous view. Of course, our cameras were all out of reach a few feet back in the rucksacks, but that moment's vision of the great bird will stay with me for ever. No such joy awaited me this day, but the immense drop at my feet and the sense of the great rock buttresses swelling out below were as exhilarating as before.

I had to retrace my steps before descending to the bealach at the head of the big southern corrie. I remembered that on hot days in the past we had looked out anxiously for the springs that are to be found on the steep slopes here, and I searched for them again. I drank a very little of their ice-cold water, more for old times' sake than because of any heat, but was glad that I had stopped to look at them. The water that issues from the springs is just a trickle, but it runs clear on a bed of pink sand with here and there patches of dark moss. The turf on either side is short and a vivid fresh green, and at this time of year was bejewelled with the flowers of starry saxifrage; each tiny flower a thing of beauty, with an orange spot at the base of each white petal.

So far, I had felt fit and active, but the steep ascent of the narrow crest of Creag na h-Iolaire Ard – the high rock of the eagle – slowed me a little. I did, however, enjoy it as much as ever. For me, the last two peaks (as climbed from the north) were always a fitting climax to a great hill day. The final summit, Spidean Coinnich, is also fine and shows, too, the colours of both rock types. Again, the cold prevented me from enjoying it all at leisure and I soon turned on my heel and retraced my steps to the base of the big Bealach a' Chornaidh. From here, a steep, stony descent to the west takes one down to the headwaters of the glen that would eventually lead me back to the road and my car.

Initially, however, I followed the old track that makes its way beside the burn to the first and larger loch. Down here, below the imposing line of cliffs, it was warmer and I could wander at leisure, stopping to watch two cackling red-throated divers flying past, and a dipper in the burn. I sat down on the very narrow sandy beach at the back of the loch and was taking out my thermos for a teatime cup, when my eye was drawn to a crag on my left. The binoculars revealed an immature eagle, all stark black and white, posed arrogantly on his rock, looking towards the mountain to which, eventually, he flew.

After tea, I walked by the second loch and followed the burn that issues from it. This is the same burn that had murmured its way past the gable of our cottage many years ago and every inch of it was familiar to me. It plunges merrily on its way, following one of those lines of weakness in the old Lewisian landscape. At first, there are no trees, just the outcrops of rock, deergrass, some heather where it is drier, and the burn itself – white over the falls and rapids, peaty and black in the pools. After some distance, it changes character abruptly and meanders through slow and impenetrably dark pools in what may at one time have been a lake-basin: still, sombre and at times sinister under a high, wooded crag. There are old walls here and the place is called Ruigh Dorch, 'the dark sheiling'. The black pools have always fascinated and repelled me and I decided now that I should pluck up all my adult courage and swim in one of them. So I stripped and, not without some misgiving, let myself cautiously into the water which was, at least, far less cold than I had expected. No water-horse, or indeed anything else, arose from the depths to reward my foolhardiness and I swam across the dark pool of my childhood's fears. Reinvigorated, I dressed and walked briskly back to the car.

4: Clothing the Land

THE COMING OF VEGETATION,
AND ITS SUBSEQUENT HISTORY

Tourist brochures all too often claim that the North and West is 'one of the last unspoilt wildernesses', where nature may be seen in a pristine state. Conservationists, on the other hand, often go to the other extreme, maintaining that the whole region has been degraded and devastated by man; that it is now almost completely devoid of natural qualities. Neither point of view has much to recommend it; such simple generalisations often miss the whole truth, but separating fact from fiction is equally difficult.

The last ice-sheet probably melted about 11,000 BC. At this stage, the landscape was treeless, with the probable exception of some birch in the south-west. However, it seems that even this location was limited by exposure to westerly winds. Over much of the area, scrub, with significant amounts of juniper and heathland, predominated.

Round about 9000 BC, the temperature plummeted, perhaps in response to a change in the direction of drainage of icy meltwater from the North American ice-cap. This rapid downward turn in temperature caused the renewed development of valley glaciers, creating many of the glaciated forms we see today. Around these centres of ice production the climate was, obviously, very cold, with constant freezing at night and thawing during the day. This caused active erosion and disturbed soils.

Again there followed rapid fluctuations in temperature – this time in the other direction – creating in the North East Atlantic some of the most volatile changes of average temperature seen in the history of the world. As the climate progressed towards warmer and drier conditions, so the local vegetation changed in consequence, but it is important to remember that the graph of the temperature change followed a curve. The cold conditions which had caused the re-advance of the glaciers were followed, not immediately by warm and dry conditions, but by less cold and wet weather. Under such conditions of high rainfall and low summer temperatures (as are currently experienced in this area), there is very little evaporation – the rainwater stays on, or in, the ground, which ultimately will waterlog. One effect of the high rainfall is to wash mineral salts down through the soil to its base where they form an impermeable layer called the 'Iron-pan'. This may be seen in roadside cuttings, for instance, as an orange layer. These consolidated mineral salts prevent drainage, causing the soil to waterlog. Without adequate oxygen, plant matter cannot decay completely and slowly builds up as layers of saturated peat. These acidic conditions are only hospitable to a number of specialised plants. One important member of this group of plants is sphagnum moss (in effect a vegetable sponge) which, as it grows upward, raises the water table of a healthy bog. As the climate slowly began to improve after about 8000 BC, peat did begin to form in this way and such very old peats have been found, for instance, in Shetland and in the Flow Country of Caithness and Sutherland. There is no doubt, however, that peats of this age, in whatever wasted form, must exist in many places throughout the Highlands and Islands. It is important to note that there can be no question of the development of such peats being caused or accelerated by the activities of man. We have only the most limited evidence for the presence of man anywhere in this area at this stage, and certainly not in such numbers as could have had any such significant effect on the landscape.

The nature and structure of the local rock is a most important aspect in determining what areas will waterlog and when. Some rocks as already mentioned are like limestone, free-draining to the

extent that very little peat ever forms on them. Others, especially
the masses of Torridonian Sandstone at lower altitudes, do form a
very effective barrier to the drainage of surface water and waterlog
rapidly. The contorted structure of the metamorphic rocks provides
many small basins where peat may have started to form very early
on.

As the climate improved, the tundra-like heath gave way to
drier heathland, then to juniper scrub, and then, about 7000 BC, to
hazel and birch woodlands. This woodland is often thought of as
extensive, dense and even forest but, on the contrary, it is clear that
at this stage there were considerable variations in the type and
extent of woodland cover all over the Highlands and Islands. It is
evident, for instance, that Orkney, Shetland and even central
Caithness never had extensive, consistent tree cover; the most these
areas ever seem to have had was a predominantly birch and hazel
scrub in the more sheltered spots. In Rum, too, the available
evidence does not support the idea of continuous forest. As the
soils of these areas do vary significantly (Orkney and part of
Caithness have a naturally fertile soil deriving from the Old Red
Sandstone), climatic severity is seen as the likely cause of this lack
of tree cover. In particular, high rainfall, high winds (often salt-
laden and inimical to tree growth) and the lack of summer warmth,
all cause low-evaporation rates, as already noted. This does
emphasise the importance of topographical and climatic factors in
the distribution of natural woodland.

In the wetter west especially, there can be no doubt that geology
is important in the retention of trees, and a classic site in this regard
is the major glen which runs down to Loch Kishorn (what might
be termed 'Glen Kishorn') in Wester Ross. Stand, looking
upstream, on the bridge over the river, close by Tornapress, with the
Torridonian Sandstone that leads up to the spectacular precipices
and corries of Beinn Bhan on your left. On your right, the rock is
limestone and, in complete contrast to the bare sandstone, it still has
a moderate cover of fine ash trees – indeed, further up the glen on
this side an area is managed as a National Nature Reserve. Down
here at the bridge, however, there are no deer-fences or other

barriers to keep out grazing animals, and both sheep and deer are attracted to its sweet, green turf. Despite being as open, therefore, to grazing as the sandstone on the other side of the river, it is the free-draining limestone that has retained its trees. There is obviously no significant climatic difference from one side of the glen to the other, it is simply the geology that has encouraged the retention here of the native woodland.

Very few generalisations about the subsequent history of the woodlands of our area hold fast. Detailed studies from three sites in Skye alone show how varied was the vegetational history of just this one island, and each site has relevance for other parts of the North and West.

Loch Cleat is in the north of Skye, on the Trotternish peninsula, an area that comprises lava resting on earlier sediments (the weight of the lava on the collapsing sediments is the cause of the dramatic landslide landscape of the Quirang). This rock can be relatively free-draining, but the plateau-like landscape does tend towards waterlogging on the considerable level expanses and it is also open to winds. From as early as 7000 BC (again before human intervention is likely) there were significant areas of grassland between patches of birch and willow scrub. By 6000 BC, such grassland was locally frequent and so it remained for the next 3,000 years, although the scrub acquired rowan, willow and bird cherry. It was, therefore, to an already significantly open landscape that the first farmers were attracted from about 3000 BC. No doubt their agriculture, which seems to have been largely arable, hastened the decline of the scrub, but this process does seem to have been firmly underway a lot earlier. For the last seven hundred years the landscape has been virtually treeless with abundant meadows and, formerly, much cultivation of cereals.

Between Broadford and Kyleakin, adjoining large expanses of
Torridonian, is Loch Ashik. Around 7000 BC it had woodland
(rather than the scrub of the more exposed north), with willow,
rowan and bird cherry. Over the next several thousand years, oak
and ash waxed and waned in importance, and some heaths,
grasslands and bogs appeared, but it seems clear that these latter
were in response to natural changes, rather than in any way
connected with man's activities.

Around 3000 BC, during a period of climatic optimum with
warmer and drier conditions prevailing than those we currently
enjoy, there was, interestingly, no evidence of agriculture or of
significant clearance of woodland. There was, rather, an increase in
the amount of pine and it has been suggested that the Scots pine
(which is here at the western-most part of its range) was finding
suitable growing conditions on the surface of peat bogs which had
dried out in the warmer weather. This lasted till about 2000 BC,
with the onset of cooler and wetter conditions.

The increased waterlogging then caused the formation of more
heaths and bogs (which are, as already noted, prone to form on the
Torridonian) and seems effectively to have killed off the pine, while
at the same time reducing the area of birchwoods. In the
succeeding years some oak and alder came and largely went, but it
is clear that the landscape around Loch Ashik, boggy and virtually
treeless as it is, appears to have changed very little in the last 3,000
years. Nor does it appear that the history of this landscape shows
much response to the hand of man through the ages.

The third site is Loch Meodal, on the road over to Ord, in Sleat.
This loch is situated on a very boggy plateau, but is not far from
birch woodlands to its west. This whole area appears to have
retained its predominantly wooded nature for much longer than
the other sites. In this context it should be noted that the
surrounding topography, particularly on the west, is more broken-
up than that of the others, offering shelter and some steep, free-

draining slopes. Right up into the early centuries AD, the landscape seems to have remained one of birch, hazel and alder woods, with frequent grasslands, heaths and occasional bogs. The most dramatic change in this area appears only to have come in the last 300 years, with considerable deforestation and a real increase in the area of bog and grassland.

One of the many interesting conclusions that may be drawn from this study of Loch Meodal is that the patches of woodland that are still to be seen in Sleat are, in fact, remnants of the native forest, of the Scottish 'Wildwood', if you like. While some of them may be secondary growth after felling, there are places, for example around Ord, which do give an idea of the richness and variety of this deciduous forest. One characteristic is its diversity – there is birch, rowan, various willows, alder, hazel, oak, ash, wych elm, bird cherry, holly and hawthorn; with bushes of wild rose, juniper, occasional elder, blackthorn and, more rarely, guelder rose, sometimes draped with ivy or honeysuckle.

The woodland wildflowers of bluebell, wood anemone and wild garlic (or ramsons) are common (and make a spectacular spring show around Armadale), but there may also be found in places, sanicle and woodruff, which seem to be characteristic of undisturbed natural woodland. Such woods are rich in ferns, lichens, mosses and liverworts, but many also have extensive areas of bracken, an invasive species that can now grow so densely that it inhibits the growth of seedling trees.

Contrary to frequent expectation, many of these patches of coastal woodland (which may be found all the way up the west) are in good health, despite the numbers of sheep and deer which often graze in them. A study of such woods in Assynt has identified that it is further inland, and over an altitude of about 100 metres, that the most vulnerable woods are located. In inland Assynt substantial areas of woodland around Elphin disappeared between 1774 and the present, but that trend is far less marked along the coast, where there has indeed been some local expansion. Again, climatic factors may be implicated here.

In some exposed areas, as high on the Sgurr of Eigg or in certain parts of Orkney like Durkadale, the natural vegetation appears to consist of large mounds of willow. In the very sheltered glen of Berriedale in Hoy occurs the most northerly natural woodland in Britain, with willow, birch, aspen, hazel and rowan, but there is also aspen on the Scapa Flow coast. Experience of tree-growing in Orkney makes it quite clear that shelter is a most significant aspect. Salt-laden winds kill trees very effectively, as anyone who has tried to grow them in an exposed location can vouch, and evergreens in particular may fare very badly in winter gales. In windy winters, salt spray has been found on the windows of houses at least ten miles from the coast and plantations of conifers, like those now growing around Loch Craggie above the Oykell, show for many months after the effect of the blasting that they receive during the cold months.

It is precisely the effect of this exposure, of course, which favours the growth of prostrate shrubs like creeping willow or flowers that would elsewhere be regarded as alpine, being found nearer and nearer to sea level as one progresses northwards.

Heading back down the east coast towards Inverness, pockets of native woodland still survive in this more agricultural area. The Mound Alderwoods are of particular interest in that they only developed since the Mound itself was constructed by Thomas Telford in 1813. The Fairy Glen and Drummondreach Woods in the Black Isle are important remnants, rich in wild flowers, including woodruff, wood- and water-avens, and the minute moschatel.

Especially in the catchment of the River Glass, but found elsewhere in the North and West, are the remaining areas of Caledonian Pine Forest – fine stands of those pines which appeared and then disappeared soon afterwards around Loch Ashik in Skye. Especially in spring or autumn, when the dark green of the red-barked pines is contrasted with the brilliant leaves of birch and aspen, these are the most beautiful woodlands, home to a specialised if sometimes elusive wildlife, which include the capercaillie, Scottish crossbill and crested tit. Healthy pine woods have a rich understorey of heather (mainly ling), juniper, blaeberry and cowberry. Strathfarrar may well be considered by connoisseurs to be the loveliest of such woods. Even in these Caledonian Pine woods, the pine is merely the dominant tree, there will also be birch, rowan, willow, aspen, hazel and, depending on soils, perhaps oak as well.

As one moves down the Great Glen, oak comes more and more into prominence, and is a major feature of the fine woods that remain on the former Clanranald Estate lands between Morar and Ardnamurchan.

Contrary to popular belief, many of these surviving areas have, in fact, experienced considerable exploitation in the past. Loch Maree, for instance, is a well-wooded and lovely loch, but it is also known that its woods were used to make charcoal for a local iron-smelting industry. Logging may often create, in the very churned-up mess of timber extraction, ideal conditions for the growth of new seedlings. There is also evidence that coppicing and pollarding, sophisticated forms of woodland management, permitting harvesting over a prolonged period, took place in some localities in the Highlands. Fire is often referred to as an agent of destruction, but it is only that if done repeatedly, as in the regular heather burning of the east coast (for purposes of grouse management), or when followed by heavy grazing, as in the sheep-rearing areas of the west.

There can be no doubt that the cooler, wetter periods in our history – during the Bronze Age, for example, or from *c.*1500-1750 AD (known as the Little Ice Age) – would have had a significant effect in limiting the regeneration of trees. But apart from these climatic effects, and from any activities of mankind, other natural factors have had a considerable influence on the vegetation of the Highlands and Islands.

Recently we have come to realise that the regular and major eruptions of Hekla in Iceland are likely to have had a dramatic impact on the Highland environment through thousands of years. The great quantities of ash and dust thrown high into the atmosphere will have had the obvious effect of creating cloud systems and inaugurating spells of colder weather, but equally or more dramatic will have been the result of the deposition of the often toxic chemicals contained in those clouds. The combination may have at its worst been inimical to vegetation and may, for instance, have caused the disappearance of pine from Caithness in about 1850 BC. The effect on the human population and their livestock is likely to have been at times equally catastrophic, and one cannot be certain that any part of the North and West will have escaped such devastation at some stage in their long history.

The present aspect of the Highlands and Islands is the result of a long and complicated evolution through time, at the mercy of a whole range of factors of which man has been only one.

5: Assynt

STOER POINT

The day before I climbed Quinag had begun very cloudy, with the mountains hidden, and I had followed the narrow road through the rough gneiss country north of Lochinver, with no clear idea of where I was heading. Once out at Clachtoll I could see that it was lightening in the west and I decided that it was sensible to head towards that light, so I made for the Point of Stoer. The Point itself may be approached from two sides, and I took the more northerly via Culkein Stoer (Culkein is *cul-chinn*, 'the back of the head' or 'headland').

As one reaches Stoer itself, it becomes apparent that the road, for a while, approximates to a geological boundary – over to the east is the rough, hummocky Lewisian landscape, but to the west the ground is significantly smoother.

My road left the 'main' road at Loch Neil Bhain, a loch whose backdrop, as it were, shows the structure of this part of the country in remarkably clear fashion. The loch lies at the foot of a narrow glen between ridges, which themselves consist of obviously inclined strata. The clue to the nature of the rock is given by the dark purple stone of Stoer Primary School, attractively situated by the loch; the rock of Stoer is Torridonian.

My way took me down to the bay of Culkein, with wide views northwards over Eddrachillis to Handa, the famous bird sanctuary, whose cliffs are formed of the same rock. Culkein Bay has an attractive sweep of sand that extends almost as far as the stone pier.

Behind the beach there are large smooth fields, many delineated by stone dykes, and behind these the cliffs of the headland itself appear. The eye is drawn along the shore, past the pier to the first small headland which terminates in a fine natural arch. I left the car and walked beside a substantial stone wall, which had collapsed in only a few places, to the cropped turf of this first promontory. This has been at one time utilised as a fort and the headland is cut across by the remains of a strong wall of large boulders. The entrance passage can still be made out. Beyond the narrowest neck of land, just at the arch itself, a few courses of stone remain to indicate that a structure stood here on the very cliff edge – as draughty a location as one could find.

The cliffs westward slowly gain height and I walked along them, looking over the smooth contours to the south. Stoer Point is very different from the rest of Assynt and reminds me a bit of Orkney with its precisely-drawn cliffs. However, the fields behind the walls were most unlike Orkney in only containing sheep and being, in places, badly overgrown with rushes.

The cliffs have plenty of ledges which provide ideal nesting places for seabirds. The birds here seem to operate some sort of ghetto system. At first, I went through a clearly defined territory of gulls before getting to the area occupied by the fulmars. These I find attractive; they appear inquisitive about us and as they glide on stiff wings along the cliff edge will come closer and closer, until you can see clearly the complicated bill and large dark eyes. They are magnificent fliers and take a visible delight in riding the updraughts along the cliffs. Their offspring were sitting by themselves, large splodges of down with a bill and two eyes, on ledges surrounded by gardens of late thrift and the succulent roseroot. Beyond the fields, the bog inland reaches close to the cliff-edge, but outwith the fence (and so out of reach of the sheep), on the very brink where it is also driest, there was prolific growth, with the rich crimson flowers of the bell heather now in full bloom. Here and there were the small golden flowers of the ubiquitous tormentil.

There is a large bay in an angle of the eastern cliffs and on reaching its head I realised that there was actually a feasible, if steep, grassy route down to a tiny beach amid large boulders at the foot of the cliffs along which I had come. Partly because a brisk wind had sprung up, I decided to descend to sea level, and this I gingerly did. Here, I stopped and had lunch and, rather vaguely, paddled, but the water was too chilly and I soon gave up. I watched a cruise ship from the north sail into and out of view, and the heads of a few Atlantic seals appear and disappear in the waves. The sound of the surf was regular and hypnotic, and down here, out of the wind, the sun, which had duly emerged, was warm. I sat on a boulder, pondered on nothing, and very nearly fell asleep.

Eventually I came to and heaved my way back up to the clifftop. I debated whether to cross the boggy heights of the peninsula in order to get a glimpse of the famous Old Man of Stoer, a remarkable and somewhat topheavy rock-stack, but as I had in mind to visit another place, I returned to the car.

Once back on the main road, I took a familiar route; first of all to Clashnessie with its fine waterfall and pink sands, and then eastwards over rock and water past Oldany to Drumbeg. The road twists and turns, providing marvellous glimpses of the sea, the islands and, of course, the mountains; yet always progressing through increasingly more wooded hollows and small glens. Some of the many lochs around Drumbeg provide good trout fishing and no doubt the feeding in the best of them is much enhanced by the numbers of insects and caterpillars that are associated with the birch woods in summer.

The next part of the drive, from Drumbeg towards Kylesku, was pure nostalgia, as I passed the cottage which had been ours for so many years, and many other familiar landmarks, all dominated by that magical, memory-imprinted outline of Quinag. I had decided to go looking again for an ancient monument which I knew from old times. As I remembered, it was close to the road, but I had only visited it once or twice in the past and thought it would be fun to try to find it again. I knew well enough where to look: as the road climbs out of what had been 'our' glen, it passes an area of tumbled low walls, which is all that remains of the original village. This being high summer, the walls were for the most part obscured by bracken and I kept on falling over unseen stones. Eventually I reached the small burn, which I knew meant that I was close to what I sought and I cast around among the birches. For a while I found nothing and although the burn seemed familiar, something about its surroundings seemed rather different. I slowly discerned (and a subsequent look at old photos confirmed this) that when I had first explored here, it was an area of young scrub birch. These had grown into virtually mature trees, dramatically altering the scale of the entire place. In order to find out exactly where I was I had to go further out into the open to a fine viewpoint above the deep glen with its glinting river. From there I could make my way back from that known point towards the road.

Suddenly I saw what I was looking for although, truth to tell, it would be easy enough to go straight past it. Virtually hidden in the bracken and at some distance from each other, are two moss-covered, roughly horizontal boulders. One in particular hints of a void under it and, if you lie down, pushing your head into the hole and inching forward, you become aware of the remains of quite a large chamber under the ground. I had, by chance, a torch in the car (and the batteries were still working!) and its light showed clearly the roof, made of hefty stone lintels, and the drystone walls. The original floor is quite obscured now, by water apart from anything else. The long subterranean chamber has succeeded in catching the waters of a tiny stream and has thereby converted itself into a remarkably elaborate drain, which was certainly not its original purpose! Such underground structures (sometimes called 'souterrains' or 'earth-houses') were almost certainly built for storage and are likely to have been associated with buildings on the surface, which have often since disappeared. I walked round and round in the bracken, looking for traces of some such contemporary surface structure. Finding nothing, I eventually retreated to the car, pursued by a crowd of midges that had suddenly appeared; the brisk wind, tantalisingly, having suddenly dropped away to nothing.

6: Patterns in the Land

THE INFLUENCE OF CLIMATE

To those who look at the land of the North and West (and some visitors may not see further than the outline of the scenery), the surface of much of that land appears as a series of unexplained splodges of colour, especially in the winter. Writing now on a beautiful but brisk day in February, the 'splodginess' of the landscape contrasts strongly with the clear, delicate sweep of the unclouded sky and the flash of the brilliant sea. Of course, much of the surface of the land is bare rock, although even it, as we have seen, varies in colour. But much of the rest – part of its joy to those who love it, whatever the weather – is an apparently inconsequential pattern of colours. The dark, rich brown, so strong in winter, denotes an area of thick heather growing on relatively dry ground; of Scotland's three native heathers, only the cross-leaved heath can tolerate much water around it. Ling and bell heather only flourish where it is dry. The real unbroken sweeps of heather are thus found to the east, where it is drier; here there may be splodges too, but these are likely to be the result of frequent, local burning to create differential growth for grouse habitat.

In the winter, wetter ground will have less heather, and its grasses and sedges will range from yellow ochre to tawny in colour. Small, vivid green splodges at this time of year are likely to be very damp patches, perhaps around springs, where the sphagnum moss grows. In the wetter west, however, short grass may grow green all through the winter, given the stony (and therefore better drained) foundations of old field walls and buildings. Sometimes bracken will follow these as well, as it likes dry ground, often that formerly occupied by woodland, where in the winter its dead stalks and leaves provide (for all that it is a real pest) a rich rust colour which adds brilliance to the scene. The birches, especially the younger ones, are a cloud of reddish purple, which lasts until new leaf is about to appear in the spring.

It is in the late autumn, after the last leaves have gone from the trees, that the deergrass of the west comes into its own, glowing a deep and rich red. But by the spring, such moors are monochrome and dead-looking, in places as black as the peat underneath them. Anyone who has cut peat by hand will know that it is almost as much liquid as solid. That applies also to the moors composed of such peat.

On the edge of a level moor, where the ground falls away in steeper slopes, you may see the peat crack where it thins and, under the influence of gravity and all the water that it contains, start, infinitely slowly, to move downhill, in a way that is slightly reminiscent of a thin, 'ironed out' glacier. Like a glacier, too, it can develop subterranean drainage as some of the water it contains begins to flow over the bedrock beneath. Eventually, such internal erosion in the peat can open up sink-holes, which may often be seen on level moors. Sometimes, the roof of these subterranean channels may collapse, creating a deep gully which is then open to erosion. This could explain some of the fearsome peat hags that are to be encountered in the higher reaches of this area. Fire, and the passage of thousands of sharp-footed sheep and deer contribute, but their origin is likely to have been natural.

Looking at this sort of landscape, it is easy to believe that it is static. However, as we have seen in the case of the peat, that is really not so; in some cases, peat is still forming. Neither are soils fixed and static; particularly in Scotland's climate, they are continually evolving and changing. Soils are initially the product of the parent rock and it has already been noted that much of Scotand's geology is unpromising in this regard. Torridonian Sandstone, for instance, weathers to form a sand consisting mostly of grains of quartzite, of which the most positive thing that can be said is that it will at least promote drainage. Access to minerals is fundamental and soils begin to form where these are readily available, perhaps where areas of rock are breaking down naturally. This may be where scree or fallen rock is crumbling, perhaps at the foot of cliffs – and this is referred to as a 'dry flush' – or where spring water brings minerals to the surface. This latter is known as a 'wet flush' and the springs from which I drank high on Quinag are a good example.

As has been explained, the degree of waterlogging depends both on relief and climate, and this is a crucial factor in determining the profile of the soil that develops. The nature of a soil both influences, and is influenced by, its vegetation. The native deciduous trees will grow where they have access to the minerals they need – as on steep, well-drained slopes – but they make their own contribution to the development of the soil. Their deep roots seek out the minerals and organic matter that have been washed into the lower layers of the soil (and the minerals from the bedrock), while their fallen leaves effectively return those minerals to the upper levels of soil in the autumn.

If the trees were not there, even on relatively steep slopes, our high rainfall would have the inevitable effect of washing out – or 'leaching' – the minerals and organic matter of the soil. In flatter areas this leads rapidly to waterlogging and the formation of bogs.

Areas of bog play an effective part in limiting the possibilities of woodland regeneration. Trees, with the exception of alders and some willows, cannot grow well with their roots in water. In some places, such as the small but jewel-like Coire Loch in Glen Affric, or in the remarkable wilderness of the Monadh Mor in the Black Isle, tiny pines may be seen in check, surviving but not growing in the wet ground adjoining the open water. The problem is that the seedlings of many of our native deciduous trees, especially the birch, do not grow in the deep shade cast by their parents. When that group of elderly trees dies off, they stop taking up water from the ground and their roots decay; the surrounding bog invades, takes over the patch of now fallow ground, denying it to a succeeding generation. With the high rainfall that this area experiences, this may happen relatively rapidly, leading to a natural fragmentation and 'islanding' of much of the native woodland.

Above all, it becomes clear that this is not a static landscape, it is rather one of movement and change. It would be so even if man had never set foot here. Different cycles of change are at work all around us. Those ancient rocks which eroded to form sand and mud over millions of years were reconsolidated to form rock again, and are now, once again, at the Point of Stoer, being pounded into sand. The glaciers dug deep trenches, such as Strath Glass, into the landscape. Nature, with infinite patience and over a timescale that mocks our transience, is working to reduce the sharp edges of such deep glens, and ultimately to fill them. She is working to level the highest mountains and with the material taken from them, to fill the deepest seas. On a much shorter timescale, woods have moved into zones of shelter, their young growth following the seeds picked up by the prevailing winds, their rearguard harried by salt spray.

Slightly less fundamental changes, but both serious and long-lasting, can also happen quite quickly in this climate. Where arable land ceases to be worked, it rapidly reverts to a jungle of bracken, if dry, or rushes if wet. The clearance of both is a major operation. I have seen fields which produced good crops of oats or hay revert to a mass of rushes in less than 20 years. 'Use it or lose it' is a good maxim for arable land in the Highlands and Islands.

Instability, too, is now a major feature of the climate, of which already quite a lot has been said. Certain generalisations can be made: it is generally cool, wet and windy like all maritime climates, but towards the east it takes on some characteristics of the drier continental climate. But these are average conditions and what has been most noticeable in recent years, east and west, has been its unsettled nature. The weeks or months of deep snow or hard frost that the eastern glens used to experience have become uncommon. Depressions track constantly across the Atlantic, often bringing high winds. Some bring down cold air from the Arctic and we have snow. The next day, another brings mild air from the Azores, and the thaw sets in, causing flooding. A brief ridge of high pressure brings frost and black ice, but two days later the wind is howling again and rain is streaming across the country. Spring, for some years, almost totally disappeared, but recently has made something of a comeback, while summers have tended to be dull. But you never can tell: writing in early 2003, we have had the most wonderful and sunny autumn and winter I can ever recall!

The reasons for such unstable conditions are outside the consideration of this book, but they are certainly hard on man and beast, probably not good even for deciduous vegetation, let alone evergreen, and must have a serious effect on soils. Constant waterlogging, for instance, has been a notable feature of many winters.

But these harsh conditions of which we all complain, these same winds before which we quail, have helped to create one of our greatest marvels. All along the Scottish west coast prevailing winds pound at the cliffs and smash into fragments the shells of countless marine organisms. The resulting shell-sand creates the breath-taking beaches of the west, and it is also rich in calcium. It sweetens the acid soils on to which it is blown and where not overgrazed or flattened and torn by cars, caravans and tents, supports a magnificent richness of wild flowers, which has to be seen to be believed. This is the Hebridean machair and although many of the flowers that grow in it – like red clover and lady's bedstraw – are quite common elsewhere, here they grow in a scented profusion that creates a startling contrast with the bare hills of gneiss a few miles further east.

7: Loch Affric

We hadn't even started to walk today before there was a great deal of excitement. We were driving along slowly when, just before we got to the car park, where the individual, old Scots Pines begin, a large bird flew out of the heather and up into a tree. There it perched, obligingly visible on a branch but, awkwardly, right against the light. The only way to see any colour on it at all was to walk a considerable distance along the road and view it from one side. That it was female and a member of the grouse family we agreed, but what started us arguing was that we had no real sense of scale. There wasn't a thing in sight, certainly not another bird (how often this is the case!), by which to measure it, and although we desperately wanted it to be a female capercaillie, we were all serious enough ornithologists (or pretended to be) to feel that we had to consider the possibility that it might be a greyhen (a female black grouse). The male caper, nearly as big as a turkey, is spectacular and unmistakable, but the female is smaller and comparatively drab, though on closer inspection her plumage is a rich and varied brown. Eventually, we decided that our mysterious bird, dark against the sun, was a capercaillie and so, greatly pleased, we proceeded to the car park.

Loch Affric lies roughly midway across the Northern Highlands, with a fine range of mountains to the north and lesser hills to the south. The loch itself by no means lies at the head of its glen, which continues as far as the watershed, located, as usual, not far from the western seaboard. Many such long glens or linked glens lead through the mountains of the Highlands, but Affric must be one of the most beautiful. Its chief claim to fame is that it contains one of the most significant remnants of the native Pine Forest, grouped around two lovely lochs.

We had decided to walk along the north shore of Loch Affric and the first section is in effect the drive of the fine Victorian shooting lodge. This is situated some distance along the north shore, at a point where the loch contracts to narrows that are bridged. The day was calm and this first part of the loch mirrored the deep colours of the dark pinewood on the southern shore, gashed here and there by the sunlight on the brilliant green of new birch leaves. There was a heron on our shore, silhouetted, unmoving, one of those birds with which one is familiar but which, through the binoculars, looks fantastical, alien, unreal. In complete contrast, a clear call from some birch scrub announced the presence of a willow warbler, a welcome harbinger of our northern spring. A sleek shape on the water, with tip-tilted bill, was a red-throated diver; a cuckoo called close by; and a fluttering of wings on a stony beach revealed a common sandpiper – we were doing well!

Once past the lodge and on the path proper, we settled down to walking. At this point the pinewood is very open, almost too open to be called a wood, just a number of old pines growing in the heather. The foundations of a number of old buildings make it clear that this area has been inhabited for a few hundred years at least. The hills high above us were white with snow and overall there arched a clear blue sky at which I peered at regular intervals, supposedly in the hope of seeing an eagle, though in fact I had never done so here.

We did see plenty of red deer, all stags, scraggy and scruffy after the winter. Most had lost their antlers and some were visibly regrowing them under the protective skin that is called velvet. This annual regrowing is a cruel drain on the beast's resources, just at the time when it is at its weakest after the winter. Although they were shy of our party, they lacked the energy or the inclination to move far from the spot where the keeper would be feeding them, supplementing the sparse diet they could get from the bare hill. April is in some ways the hardest time of the year for them. However green the deep glens may be becoming, on the open hill it might almost as well be winter: very little has started to grow. As though to prove the point, as we walked a breeze sprang up and clouds came out of the west, it grew cold and soon there were snowflakes on the breeze, which grew to be a wind and swirled among the trees.

Pulling on hats and gloves, and doing up coats, we plodded on against the weather. The path crosses a number of burns with splashy falls, dark pools and amber-coloured shallows, and it was close to one of the largest of these that we decided to stop and have lunch while we still had the protection of a number of trees. In fact, we had little need of shelter as the shower soon passed over, the sun came out and the fallen snow immediately began to melt. All the trees now began to drip, so lunch was an awkward affair. Those who had halted under the trees moved out rapidly – the ground was too sodden for anyone to want to sit on it – so some stood around uncomfortably, eating their sandwiches. Those of us who had sat down on the available boulders might have been considered to be better off as the sun was now warm, but the boulders were chill to our behinds, so lunch was brief and we were soon again on the move.

We were now in open ground, approaching a smaller loch along a more level but very boggy path. Beyond this, the route climbs a small hill before descending to the broad river that flows into Loch Affric. Here, it used to be crossed by an old suspension bridge and we had intended to return along the Forestry road on the southern side. We had, however, been warned at the car park that the bridge had been destroyed in a winter flood (it has since been rebuilt) and, as the weather was again worsening, we decided to call a halt and return the way we had come.

We were with a party of schoolchildren, whose spirits notably improved as we changed direction and had our backs to the wind. They became increasingly noisy as we returned to the trees.

Eventually, I had had enough of the row. I sat them down under a fine spreading 'granny' pine and told them to keep quiet so that we could listen to what was going on around us. In the silence, I almost immediately heard the call of a crested tit, which came closer and closer. Suddenly it was visible, near to us, and we had a splendid view as it flew into a crack in a dead and rotting tree only a few feet from us. For a while we watched this dapper and special inhabitant of the Caledonian Pine Forest flitting to and from its nest. It was so close that binoculars were almost unnecessary.

Back at the foot of the loch we crossed the Forestry bridge and looked at a section of the wood which has been protected from the grazing of the deer. What was so noticeable here was the undergrowth – high, bushy heather; cowberry; juniper – and among them the young generation of pines which would follow the fine mature specimens that so distinguish this area. To my great pleasure we found another typical inhabitant of this forest – a tiny, delicate, star-shaped white flower called, mysteriously, 'chickweed wintergreen'. It is neither a chickweed nor a wintergreen and does not look in the least bit like either family! In general, it is to be found in pinewoods or where such woods have been, but there is at least one extraordinary exception to this generally accepted rule. I have since discovered that a few specimens grow healthily on the slopes of the Isle of Noss in Shetland, one location where one can pretty safely say there has never been a pinewood!

Once we were in the minibus we headed back to base in Strathglass. The lower strath seemed lush, green and exotic, with its blooming gean, bird cherry and sloe – almost a foreign country after a day spent walking on the shores of Loch Affric.

Below Cannich, the river meanders in its deep, fault-guided trench and we took the back road to see whether by chance any golden eye duck might still be lingering in its dark pools. We failed to see one, but were amply compensated by the clear view of a pine marten crossing the road ahead of us and vanishing into the safety of a dense plantation of conifers.

8: People Arrive

A few miles south of Inchnadamph in Assynt, in a narrow side glen, there is a fine boss of limestone rearing above the burn which is called the Allt nan Uamh. A steep green slope leads up from the waterside to the caves from which the burn takes its name. They are extensive, have long been known as the 'Bone Caves', and seem destined to remain controversial in Scottish archaeology. These caves were excavated in the 1920s and apart from the bones of animals such as lemming, arctic fox and reindeer, the excavators at the time claimed that there was also proof of contemporary human presence. That claim, discounted by archaeologists of the period, was in effect revived at the end of the 1980s but once again seems to be out of favour. There is no space here to enter this controversy. However, as it is understood that at least one site in coastal Norway has produced proof of human presence around 8000 BC, it seems possible that some Highland or Island coastal site may emerge with reliable, conclusive evidence from at least this sort of date.

At the time of writing, however, our earliest site is in an almost equally unlikely place, which indicates the danger of deducing too much from the limited evidence we have of this period. It happens that our first known group of hunter-gatherers was on the island of Rum around 6500 BC. One might assume that if they had made their way to Rum (by no means the most accessible of islands), they would be found to have been virtually everywhere else! Be that as it may, within the next 1,000 years or so there is evidence of their presence in several coastal locations: Islay, Jura, Ulva, Colonsay, Oban, Ardnamurchan, Skye (Staffin), Loch Torridon, Bettyhill, Orkney, the Cromarty Firth and Inverness. We may be talking in terms of small groups of people moving around the country in search of different, seasonally available resources, including the hazelnuts which provided the datable material from Rum. It is at least clear that some coastal sites were used over long periods, giving rise to the large shell mounds of Oronsay (by Colonsay) and elsewhere.

There has been some debate as to whether fire was used as a means of inland woodland clearance at this time but, as the total Highland population at this period is likely to have numbered no more than a few thousand, it seems evident that any such effect would be only temporary.

In this period, which has been labelled the Middle Stone Age, the only technology available to these people was that which they managed to create out of stone, wood, bone and animal skins. Any habitations, apart from caves, seem likely to have been light and temporary, and rings of stones in Jura may represent stones placed around the edges of tent-like structures, weighing down the skins that kept out the weather. We can, of course, deduce that these people had boats, whether dug-outs or coracle-like, but they must have been quite seaworthy if the Pentland Firth was crossed regularly.

By about 4000 BC or earlier a greater number of people with new skills and interests were ferrying their domestic animals across that same, sometimes turbulent, piece of water. They also crossed the Minch and, even more remarkably, reached Shetland.

These people of the New Stone Age were agriculturalists, rearing animals and growing crops. This was a period of climatic optimum; it was warmer and drier than it is now, and they seem to have flourished. Although they almost certainly started by building in wood, they were soon building substantial structures in stone. By 3500 BC they were building so well that some of their structures have survived almost intact to this day. All over the Highlands and

Islands you may find these structures, the chambered cairns. These were tombs, probably communal, and were elaborately and carefully constructed.

Orkney sandstone was laid down in thin layers, which split off easily, providing the best building stone in the Highlands and Islands. It is therefore in Orkney that we see these tombs at their best. Among the many remarkable structures here one of the last to be built, Maes Howe, has quite outstanding masonry; it is the finest building of its type in Western Europe. It is not too much to say that if we only knew for whom this great tomb had been built, it would probably figure in the popular imagination as one of the great wonders of the ancient world.

Once built, these tombs may have remained as the focus for the community ritual activities for almost a thousand years, but it was not long after 3000 BC that new and even more impressive monuments were being created in our landscapes. These are the great stone circles. Brodgar and Stenness in Orkney, and Callanish in Lewis dominate their surrounding countryside in the way that Stonehenge and Avebury do theirs in the far-off south of England. They are spectacular and may have taken hundreds of thousands of man-hours to build. Brodgar, for instance, had over sixty stones, the tallest of which is over five metres high, and a surrounding 'ditch' (more like a dry moat) which is cut down into the bedrock. It is all the more annoying, therefore, that we have no real clue as to why they were built. That those who erected them were well organised, sophisticated and skilful cannot be doubted, but what they did with or in the great stone circles remains a source of much debate. There are those who argue that they provide the means of calculating or foretelling specific astronomical events. While this argument has its attractions, it cannot explain either the excavation of the 'ditch' around Brodgar (and there was one at Stenness also), or the amazing prodigality of effort involved in such sites. This is important: the major site at Callanish would have been enough, surely, with the addition of a few more stones, to calculate nearly anything one wanted to, but the remarkable fact is that there are no fewer than twenty intervisible sites (this total includes single standing stones) in the Callanish area. Having built Stenness, why go on to build Brodgar? (And what was the Ring of Bookan?)

Shetland can provide no stone circles, but has enigmas of its own. At Stanydale there is a very large and still imposing building which has been claimed as a temple, but which could equally well have been a town hall! This remarkable structure is further notable in being surrounded by traces of the agricultural landscape that sustained the people who built it.

There are also remains here of contemporary houses. Many in Shetland are simply oval structures, although close to Stanydale 'Temple' is one that is more substantial, elongated with perhaps a porch or some sort of recess close to the doorway. Neolithic houses in the Western Isles seem again to be simple oval shapes, in real contrast to the best-known site in Orkney. Skara Brae is remarkably well preserved and so well known that it needs no further description here beyond saying that its house interiors demonstrate clearly, in stone, the level of sophistication that one may presume all, or at least some, contemporary domestic interiors possessed. Where possible, wood was no doubt used instead of stone. I have always found one feature of note and fascination far beyond even the hearths, beds and dressers so competently created of flagstone: underlying the houses of the second phase of building (sometime after 3000 BC), and certainly planned and constructed before that phase began, is a stone-built drainage system which can be accessed from some of the houses. Whether its primary purpose was to lower the water table under the newer houses or to function as a sewer (it could have been used for both) we cannot really tell. It remains, however, as a remarkable indicator of the skills available in New Stone Age Orkney.

So rich, indeed, are the remains in Orkney from this period that there may be a tendency to assume that all of the Highlands and Islands were as densely populated. It is as well to remember that Orkney has a natural fertility and probably has always been a relatively good place in which to live. Furthermore, because the agriculture which supported the builders of these monuments would have involved forest clearance (where forests existed), there is a tendency to assume that this period saw wholesale clearance of the native woodland throughout the Highlands and Islands. The evidence from the three loch sites in Skye shows just how wrong such an assumption might be (*see* chapter 4): there is equally the possibility that these farmers were attracted to places where the landscape was, by reason of exposure to winds, already open.

If the New Stone Age seems remarkably rich in spectacular monuments, its succeeding period, the Bronze Age, is very different. The chief characteristic of this period appears to be climatic decline; it slowly became colder, wetter and windier. This not only had the effect of moving people down from the higher hill land, thus freeing the land for peat to form, but forced them out of the valley bottoms which were increasingly prone to flooding. Concentration of the existing population in the middle-ground would have led to congestion, a declining standard of living and increased competition for the remaining good land.

This general decline may be mirrored in a move away from the impressive tombs to inhumation (either as simple burials with the body being folded up, or as cremations) in stone boxes called 'cists'. These were quite often placed in or near the top of artificial mounds (which, confusingly, have a variety of names such as 'barrows' or 'kerb-cairns'). These mounds are generally smaller than, and lack the complicated internal structure of, the earlier chambered tombs. Houses seem normally to have been circular, with quite thick walls, and spacious (some have an internal diameter of seven to ten metres) so that ubiquitous label 'the hut circle' is inappropriately derogatory. Surrounded by the field walls and clearance cairns which tell of their agriculture, these house groupings are to be seen in many areas, especially in central and eastern Sutherland. The mysteriously named 'burnt mounds', which can be found all over the Highlands, also belong to this period. The mounds themselves are not the remains of structures, merely the debris of contemporary cooking practice, accumulated over a long period. Stones were heated in a fire before being dropped into water contained in a large tank constructed of slabs and luted with clay. This (slowly) raised the temperature of the water until it was ready for the meat to be cooked. This would be placed in the tank and a lid (certainly in Orkney it was a stone slab) was placed on top. The process cracked the heating stones which were later chucked out, slowly creating the 'burnt mound'. The structures beside the mounds, and in which the hearths and tanks were located, generally appear fairly flimsy and the impression gained is of a relatively poor society. Conflict over agricultural land during this period may have led to the construction of the first strongholds.

The building of fortifications was certainly a characteristic of the succeeding Iron Age. Celtic tribes from the Continent brought with them a militaristic hero-culture into which the early Irish myths may give us a glimpse. The climatic decline seems to have continued for a time but, if so, it was not reflected by a paucity of structural remains. On the contrary, we have a positive embarras de richesses: in the way of fortifications, there are hill forts (some timber-laced and some the intriguingly named 'vitrified forts'); peninsular or promontory forts (like the one I visited at Culkein Stoer); and duns and brochs plastered all over the map. How some of these functioned is not really clear; the larger hill forts probably contained permanent settlements, while some small, inaccessible duns (like that on the Sgurr of Eigg) may only have been temporary refuges. Many labels are misapplied and some are revised as time passes: the 'broch' at Ardvar is now a 'dun' and may not be much more than a fortified farmhouse. There are 'ordinary' houses as well – round houses (in Orkney from about 700 BC), aisled round houses, wheelhouses and the wonderfully named 'wags' of Caithness. This list merely seems bewildering and we lack enough reliable dates to be able to sort them further. Suffice to say we have evidence for a substantial population all over the country at this time. Defence does seem to have been important, even if prestige did also play a part in the construction of these impressive monuments. The brochs, the remarkable double-walled drystone towers – of which the finest (Mousa in Shetland, Dun Carloway in Lewis, Dun Dornagail or Dundornadilla in Sutherland, Dun Troddan and Dun Telve in Gleann Beag near Glenelg) still reach ten metres and more – do appear to have been built in response to a real defensive need. At Gurness in Orkney are the remains of a broch tower in the centre of a sizeable contemporary community; the whole is surrounded by great ditches and ramparts – the prehistoric equivalent of a castle in the middle of a fortified town. At some stage, however, the need for defence became less and houses began to be built out into the ditch that had formerly protected the community. Whatever the background climatic conditions may have been, the brochs certainly look like the product of a confident and prosperous society.

Many brochs, in particular, are built in areas of good or at least reasonable agricultural land. It was presumably the produce of that agriculture that was stored in the underground chambers known as 'souterrains' or, misleadingly, 'earth-houses'. Many of these in the North and West seem to date from the Iron Age; there are, inevitably, fine examples in Orkney.

Until recently, the very visible defensive structures occupied the attention of the archaeologists and the ordinary farmhouses of the period went unnoticed or ignored. Although we are now beginning to identify and map these, it is hard to be sure of their relationship to the strongholds or to envisage them in their landscape setting. In the hinterland of Ord, in Sleat, however, a number of individual houses have been found, spaced out along the lower ground under the conspicuous, high, bare, quartzite ridge. This lower ground is composed of limestone and other free-draining sedimentary rocks, and it makes sense, especially in a period of poor climate, that this was the area that was farmed. It is very noticeable that the one area that was surveyed, and where no round house was found, is on infertile Torridonian Sandstone. Much of the agriculture of this period is likely to have been pastoral, but in nearby Ord Glen are the remains of terraces (representing an attempt to shape the hillside for maximum utilisation by plough), which may be contemporary with the recently excavated round house there.

That this area of Ord has long been settled can certainly not be doubted. It also possesses, the reader will remember (*see* chapter 4),

Ptarmigan and mountain hare may be seen on the high ridges and peaks of Quinag

Looking east across the Moine Thrust: beyond the angled, quartzite dip-slopes in the middle of the picture, mountain-building has piled up older rocks above younger. Through this complex landscape, glaciers following lines of weakness have gouged deep glens and fjord-like sea-lochs

The fertile soil of Orkney gives the landscape an unexpected lush appearance, even in winter. The islands are quite densely populated, and in areas sheltered from the worst of the salt-laden winds, trees do actually grow

The relatively soft Orkney sandstone is laid down in shallow beds, here gently inclined. Lashed by high seas in the winter, they erode very fast and form abrupt, many-ledged cliffs, which in summer provide nesting areas for seabirds, sometimes in vast colonies

one of the areas of woodland which is considered to be a remnant of the original woodland covering of Sleat. At the very least, it can be said that, under the conditions that prevail in this corner of Sleat, man and woodland have managed to co-exist since the Iron Age. It may not, surprisingly, be too implausible to venture that this could only have happened if man had been aware of the value of this woodland resource and managed it positively. This sophisticated approach to land management is clearly a possibility and not out of keeping with other skills that we know they possessed.

9: *Tom a' Choinnich*

Two friends had been going to join me on a walk this July day, but the early morning was grey and misty and they decided against it. I was all geared up to go and determined to continue with my original plans. Accordingly, I got into the car and headed up the familiar road to Glen Affric. I stopped the car by Loch Beinn a' Mheadhoin (not far from where we had seen the caper (*see* chapter 7) and set off up the track into the side glen, Gleann nam Fiadh – the glen of the deer. (The name is curious – why call any glen up here 'the glen of the deer'?) It is long, reaching far into the mountains and contains a fine, rushing burn, almost a river, which may once have flowed to the north side of Beinn a' Mheadhoin. There are indications that the large, level area between this hill and the Beinn Eun foothill of Toll Creagach was once occupied by a loch. Perhaps the eastern end of this slack ground was blocked by ice from Coire an t'Sneachda (meaning 'the coire of the snow') on the north-east face of Toll Creagach, forming a lake which then found an outlet to the south – the route now followed by the river. The burn has cut into the gravelly matter deposited in this loch and there are still some pines growing on the steep, free-draining faces so exposed. Beyond this, the landscape is treeless, an open glen under big hills.

The path goes along the burnside until it is right below the hill called 'Tom a' Choinnich' and then heads straight up. I have little liking for such vertical ascents and began slowly to ascend, going at a much gentler angle. I actually overdid it, nonetheless, and found myself higher up than I wanted to be. However, it was not unproductive as I had arrived, by chance, at the level of a long, linear, stony feature which I thought must be a lateral moraine. This, if so, is of interest in indicating the level to which the ice would have reached in the last glaciation, but the glen is wide here and the south side lower, and I was unsure of my identification.

I duly arrived at the mouth of the corrie under the south-east face of the hill and could see that my proposed summit was clear, although many others were obscured in what I hoped was thin, rather than thick, mist. I set off up the steep, elegant ridge which bounds the corrie to the south. It is rocky and some of the rocks show the shiny flakes of mica and the intense folding which is typical of the Moine schists. Eventually, the angle reduces and one starts to get one's breath back; this was needed as, despite the surrounding mist, the air was very warm. As I headed on to the plateau, the mist descended; it was not so thick that I felt unsure of the direction in which I was heading, but I did not waste any time in getting to the summit. Once there, I could not see a thing, so descended a little towards the north, disturbing one raven, until I was below the cloud level. Here I lunched and, while the mist ebbed and swirled about me, I debated what to do next. I didn't want to go home, it was far too early, and I hadn't been out long. But which way to go? There are ridges both east- and west-wards, but fate kindly stepped in and ensured that, exactly when I decided to make up my mind, the view to the east was totally obscured. The much more interesting ridges to the west – terra incognita to me – were at that moment in the sun. And so it continued. For the rest of that long day, I wandered in a clear, golden bubble, always in the brilliant sun, but surrounded by pearly mist. Hazy buttresses and peaks loomed and faded as I walked the ridges and climbed the rocky towers on that glorious afternoon. It was hot and I was lightly clad, but fleet of foot in a fabled land of enchantment and delight. Most amazing of all, I met no one else that whole day, nor was my Arcady disturbed by a single jet plane. Instead, the mournful tone of a golden plover ran for a while before me, along the moss and stones of the ridge. I was heading in the direction of the two highest hills, the highest indeed north of the Great Glen, Carn Eige and Mam Sodhail. As I approached the former, I could see that they were both totally obscured in thick cloud, so I halted. There seemed no point in climbing these two fine mountains without seeing further than the nose on my face. I lay for a while in the sun before setting off on the long descent to the head of Gleann nam Fiadh.

As I slowly made my way down, over late, fast-melting snowfields and steep grass, I came across a herd of red deer. Fortunately, they had no idea that I was close and I was able to watch them for a while. The hinds were now in truth 'red' deer, a rich and beautiful red-brown, far removed from the scruffy greyish coat of the late spring. The calves, which would have been born in June, were growing well. When eventually my presence was scented, they all began to call. It is difficult to describe the noise they made – I seem to remember Sir Frank Fraser Darling referring to the belling of the hinds, which might do, but the calves come perilously close to squeaking!

When I reached the floor of the glen I realised that down here, out of the light breeze, it was really hot. I headed promptly for the nearest deep pool and cooled off for a while, looking up to the towering ridges where, a few hours ago, I had been walking. At last I dragged myself from the water and idled down beside the burn, splashing in and out of it as I pleased. Once, a dipper flew ahead of me, looking something like a large, white-fronted bumblebee – they don't fly so much as buzz!

It was getting late, there was no one around, but it was still bright and I was in no hurry to end this wonderful day. I made my way on to the more level moor above the glen and, as I walked, looked at the bright, if tiny, flowers that starred its surface. Tormentil, of course, the deep blue of milkwort, the pink of the oddly-named lousewort. The insectivorous plants which supplement their diet by trapping insects, were coming into bloom: the violet-like flower of the butterwort above its rosette of yellow-green leaves, and the sundew with its reddish sticky pads.

Beyond the bog rises the lump-like summit of An Meallan, an unexciting hill perhaps, but a wonderful viewpoint. From it, I looked east and south over a vista of smoky-coloured moors, forests and lochs. I just sat and watched the evening steal softly over the quiet land. There was not a sound.

In the end, I dragged myself away, down the steep slope to the burn, deep amber pools under mature Scots pines. Here, too, there was no movement – at least, there was no breeze, but there were about a million midges who fastened themselves on to my exposed flesh with much delight. Once more, these tiny brutes chased me to the car, and a perfect day ended in the hysteria that only midges can bring!

10: Early History

PICTS, SCOTS, VIKINGS AND NORMANS

The Picts, who did not build the brochs, were in fact the descendants of the builders of the different types of Iron Age fortifications. They were first mentioned in 297 AD, and were the dominant force in that area of Scotland which extends from the Forth–Clyde line to Shetland and the Western Isles. They were Celtic in origin, but distinguished from their neighbours by their language which was closer to Welsh than Gaelic. They may, in fact, have spoken another language in addition: certainly there are inscriptions on standing stones which appear to be in another tongue, but which remain infuriatingly incomprehensible.

Their art was distinctive and of high quality – best known are the remarkable symbol stones with their fine and elaborate carvings. Some of the symbols are naturalistic, vigorous and stylised depictions of wolves, boars, bulls, etc; others abstract, like the crescent and V rod. There are scenes of hunting and of military exploits; later stones carry impressive crosses in high relief, and biblical scenes, with exotic animals like camels. It is thought that illustrated biblical manuscripts must have provided the sources for these. There are Pictish stones throughout most of the area, but the bulk of them are to be found around the eastern Firths (there are collections housed at Dunrobin and at Groam House in Rosemarkie). These wonderful stones present us with yet another enigma: what was their purpose? The symbols may have acted as the later clan badges did, the stones may have been territorial markers, marriage stones or have reflected some other aspect of their distinctive society which was matrilineal: although men ruled as kings, their right to do so descended through the female line.

Despite their abilities in other directions, the Picts do not seem to have excelled as builders. In places, they seem to have re-occupied hill-forts such as Craig Phadrig by Inverness, but we have so far found very few definitively Pictish houses. The best of these have (as ever!) been found in Orkney and, although not particularly well built, have an unusual plan. They are divided into compartments and the sleeping areas consist of a group of alcoves, deeply recessed around the hearth, in a trefoil or clover leaf shape.

The Picts were initially pagan, but were gradually converted to Christianity after St Columba arrived from Ireland and founded his monastery in Iona in 563 AD. He was by no means the first to cross the Irish Sea; for some centuries, the Scots had been moving across the narrow sea from Ireland and settling in the glens of Argyll, which they named Dal Riada. They must have investigated some of the long glens, especially the Great Glen, leading north and east to the fertile lands which were the centre of Pictish power. If they had territorial ambitions, the religious zeal of St Columba effectively assisted them. When he sent out his missionaries to convert the Picts, his followers would have brought as inevitable accompaniments to the Christian faith the language of the church – which was Latin – and their own Gaelic. These would have become prestigious and fashionable and would have slowly undermined the Pictish tongue. The early church could fairly be described as strongly male-oriented, which presumably threatened to undermine much that was distinctive about Pictish society.

Place-name studies help us build up a picture of the times; although a density of examples no doubt only indicates a density of population in fertile ground. The prefix 'pit' or 'pet' – meaning a share of land – is the place-name element which best defines Pictish territory. 'Kil', from 'cill' – a cell – is the Gaelic denoting an early church site, marking the inroads made by the missionaries. The Great Glen – the route used by Columba himself on his journey to see the Pictish King Bridei or Brude in his capital at or near Inverness – was no doubt a major artery of communication at that time.

Water certainly provided the lines of communication for the next people to arrive on the scene – the Vikings. They emerge dramatically into our history, making a raid on Iona in 795 AD, and repeatedly harrying the monastery there during the following years. They probably started to settle in Orkney and Shetland around this time and from there colonised the rest of the North and West until it was effectively all under their control. By the middle 800s, the Pictish kingdom, under pressure on almost all sides from Vikings and Scots, had collapsed, and the Vikings were for a while undisputed masters of the north. Place-names, especially the 'dal' (valley) names – as in Helmsdale, Obsdale – indicate the area settled by the Vikings. Although many of these are close to the coast, there are Viking names well inland, such as Alladale and Diebidale ('djupr-dal', the dark glen) in northern Ross. Another inland name is Scatwell in Strathconon, which is *skatt-vøllr* (the tax field), drawing attention to a facet of the Viking culture which is often obscured by all the accounts of rape and pillage. As well as being accomplished seafarers they were, of course, farmers, and well organised farmers at that; they devised a land-based taxation system which lasted in the north for many centuries. Administrative centres included Dingwall, whose name is related to Tynwald (Isle of Man), Tingwall (Shetland) and Thingvellir (Iceland), the first element indicating 'an assembly'. The principal centre of Norse power (Viking and Norse tend to be used somewhat interchangeably) was for a long time the tidal Brough of Birsay in Mainland Orkney, but was transferred to the growing settlement of Kirkwall. In 1137, with the foundation of St Magnus' Cathedral – that glory of the north – and of palaces for the bishop and the earl, Kirkwall became a real capital and a centre of Scandinavian culture, marking effectively the transformation of the Vikings from pagan pillagers to Christian statesmen in under four centuries.

The Vikings, of course, wandered and settled all over Europe: one group settled in northern France and, in time, these Norsemen became known as the Normans. There was no Norman conquest of Scotland, but later Scottish kings did effectively invite them into the country where they became the power base of the monarchy. Ironically, it was with the invaluable aid of these descendants of the Vikings that the Scottish crown consolidated its power and gradually extended that power northwards until by 1196 AD it had wrested control of Caithness from the Norse. In the west, Somerled, himself again a descendant of the Vikings, took control of the Isles in 1156 AD. Hakon of Norway tried to reassert his authority in 1263, but lost the decisive battle of Largs and eventually died in Kirkwall, leaving only Orkney and Shetland outwith the Scottish kingdom. It was not until 1469 that they, too, became part of Scotland but, by then, Scots influence had been growing there for many centuries.

Very generally speaking, out of this mix of Pict, Scot, Norseman and Norman, there emerged the Highland clans and the distinctive Highland culture. If Scotland's geology is complex, so too is our human history and even today the very real diversity of the cultural heritage in the Highlands and Islands is startling.

11: Orkney

Even before I left my home on the edge of the village of The Palace (named for the ruins of the elegant palace of the first Stewart Earl of Orkney), it was obvious that it was going to be a special day. A few companions and I were walking over the short, flowery turf of the Links (machair it would be in the west!) to the edge of Birsay Bay. It was already warm, promising to be significantly hot, but the day seemed, in matters meteorological, to be somewhat complex.

Despite the warmth, there was a stiff breeze from the sea and, as we began the ascent of the long, slow incline that leads up to the top of the cliffs of Marwick Head, we could see below us, in the shadow under the cliff edge, a narrow bank of thick mist. In the strong breeze, this mist continually boiled up to and over the cliff edge, only to disappear in the heat of the already brilliant sun. Slowly, it thinned, but the effect, as we gained height, of the bright sun on our left and this fog on our right, was of strange unreality.

The cliffs are principally the haunt of shag and fulmar, whose guttural conversations below us appeared fiendishly magnified by these conditions. Occasionally, a bird would emerge dramatically out of the mist, sometimes really close to us and, seemingly equally disoriented by the unusual weather, would hastily retreat into it with a loud squawk. All the while, a few yards away on our right, the calm, beautiful, enormous cows of Orkney grazed placidly on the rich grass.

As we walked further, the cloud thinned and the sounds of birdlife below us increased. There was a steady fly-past, nearly always, it seemed, from north to south, of those impressive – if not always likeable – birds, the greater black-backed gulls, and the great skuas or bonxies as they are known. Small flotillas of rapidly-flapping, torpedo-shaped auks hurtled past and as we gained the level heights of the headland and turned to face the shallow, cliff-girt bay it contains, a truly spectacular sight met our eyes.

Nothing can match the excitement, the noise, even the smell of a major seabird colony in June. Thousands of birds lined the ledges of the vertical sandstone cliff, while equal numbers appeared ceaselessly engaged in flying in and out of invisible holes in the rock face. And down there, through the fast-thinning fog, where the great rollers crashed white, were yet more birds – razorbills, guillemots, puffins, kittiwakes and fulmars, mere dots on the brilliant water hundreds of metres beneath us. I have a favourite vantage point, a natural amphitheatre seemingly quarried out to provide the perfect view along the cliffs to the tower of the Kitchener Memorial, and there we lay in safety at the cliff edge, drinking in the whole scene. Orkney's brilliant light blazed around us; the vibrant colours of sea and grass, of the drifts of sea-campion and thrift at the rock edge, and of the myriad, cascading birds completely filled our senses. It was hard to drag ourselves away, as eventually we did.

We walked along the headland, under the tower, and began the gentle descent to the southern bay, which is in fact Marwick 'proper' (wick or vik meaning a bay or harbour). The view from here southwards is over the smooth, flowing land of the West Mainland to the higher hills of Hoy with the chimney-stack feature of the famed Old Man. The day was now brilliantly clear and the whole line of the north coast of Scotland could easily be seen, with all its ranked hills – the Griams, Clibreck, Loyal (looking much more impressive than it does from the south), Hope, and the Cape Wrath hills – even the grey ridges of Foinaven.

Marwick itself is now useless as a harbour, blocked as it is by a storm beach of large boulders. The enclosed oyce provides a nice area of sheltered water, where once, when descending from the high cliffs, I saw an otter swimming. Today we were not so lucky, but there were two shelduck dames with their crèche of youngsters, some eider duck and the inevitable, noisy oystercatchers. Further to the south, in contrast to the lofty headland now left behind, the shore is low and level, at the most perhaps some 6 metres above the canted slabs of sandstone which are all that protect it from the might of the Atlantic. Despite this apparent lack of shelter, this section of the coast is not bare or eroded by the storms of winter as other parts are; on the contrary, it is well vegetated, the pale blue of spring squill now giving place to the thrift.

Eventually one comes to one of my very favourite places – the inlet of Sand Geo with its beautifully built drystone fishermen's huts and their nousts (boat-shaped depressions into which small boats were pulled to avoid being smashed in the howling gales of winter). From the huts there is a steep descent to the shore of pale grey boulders, below which is a little sand and some deep and beautiful rock pools. The water in these pools is as clear as crystal, the weeds in them many and various, coloured brilliant green, red or dark brown, and the rocky sides of the pools have a creamy-to-purple encrustation that can appear sky-blue in some lights. Here we sat or wandered and pottered about, or dozed in the warmth; it is always a comfortable place.

After a while we enjoyed a cup of tea and a discussion about the flagstones which form the roofs of the huts, then we slowly retraced our steps. It was now late afternoon, but the sun behind us was as brilliant and as warm as at midday and, rather strangely, we were apparently the only people about.

And as we walked along quietly, there leaped out of the shining ocean on our left, a pair of dolphins (we later decided that they were white-sided). As we walked, so they swam on a parallel course along the shore, regularly breaching, silhouetted against the flood of light. After the initial excitement, we became quiet, full of wonder at the beauty of the spectacle and my friends, who were older than I and less inclined to walk as fast, asked if I would like to go on at my own pace.

And so I walked alone along that magical shore, over the headland, pausing at the corner from where could be seen my old grey home, and where later the grass-of-parnassus would bloom. Behind me, the clamour of the bird cliffs; on my left the endless ocean; and, as I turned to scan the horizon, two streamlined shapes leaped once again from the depths, sending light cascading.

All the beauty of nature, all of the richness and fertility of the Orkney summer was fixed for me in that wonderful moment. Such memories sustain us through the grey and wind of winter.

12: *The Rise and Fall of the Clans*

TARTAN; THE JACOBITE RISINGS; THE CLEARANCES AND SHEEP

It is one of the ironies of history that we can describe in some detail a Pictish house, as excavated at Buckquoy, close to Birsay Bay in Orkney, or a Norse longhouse (there are several to be seen on the nearby Brough), but have difficulty in similarly depicting a typical residence of the contemporary Gaels. Despite their archaeological reticence, it was their culture, however, which was ultimately to hold sway over all the North and West, apart from the very north-east.

If Scottish history had followed the trends set by the energetic Canmore kings and their Norman adherents, the Highlands and Islands might never have achieved this cultural distinction. The prolonged struggles of the Wars of Independence following the death of Alexander III and then of the Maid of Norway, however, disrupted the process of integration and allowed the north to develop its own characteristics while the attention of the rest of Scotland was devoted to freeing itself from its southern neighbour. The Gaelic language, with its music and strong oral tradition, replaced the Norse and Pictish tongues over most of the region (place-names in Skye, for instance, often turn out to be a Gaelic veneer, as it were, over a Scandinavian layer). Highland society evolved into what is now often called the clan 'system' (although how systematic it was, I am unsure). What is certain is that the Highland clans have succeeded in weaving around themselves in the succeeding centuries a set of myths almost unmatched in the world; it is increasingly hard to find any solid ground between the dewy-eyed, tartan-swathed romantics on one hand, and the granite-hard debunkers on the other. As is so often the case, what firm facts we discover satisfy neither of these parties!

Tartan, of course, is one of the most obvious props of the enduring romance and there are some who still try to demolish its authenticity. While it is clear that many of the current tartans have only seen the light of day since that heady period when Victoria and Albert discovered the Highlands, it is by no means true of tartan itself. Old tartans exhibited in the West Highland Museum in Fort William, for instance, certainly predate the 1745 Rising. There also exist a number of paintings from shortly after 1700, such as the celebrated series of Grant portraits done by Richard Waitt, wherein a bewildering variety of setts or patterns is to be seen. Tartan clearly was worn at this time, but nothing as simple as one clan tartan is to be identified. In the 1600s, men of Mackay's Regiment, fighting for Gustavus Adolphus of Sweden, are portrayed wearing what is obviously tartan in a number of ways: mostly what we would call the belted plaid, but also what looks like a very baggy pair of breeches or plus-fours. The historian John Major, writing in 1521, stated that the 'wild Scots' wore a mantle and that their legs were bare from mid-thigh to the foot, which sounds like a possible description of the belted plaid. About this time, too, are references to 'light woollen coverings of many colours', 'variegated garments', 'plaids of many colours', and 'mottled cloaks of many colours' – so it is quite obvious that something recognisably similar to tartan has existed for centuries.

That may not be true of the kilt itself, the very practical garment which resulted when the belted plaid was divided into two portions. This may only have evolved around 1720 but, if so, it certainly proved popular and was widespread by the time of the '45 Rising.

If tartan was a distinctive accoutrement of the Highland clan, it was certainly not the only one. The bagpipe and its music has long been widely appreciated (or at least recognised) while the song and the dance of the Gael has had a rather more chequered career. Poetry has been less widely appreciated than any of these and we have no doubt lost much, although it flourished along with the telling of heroic tales, the recounting of genealogies, and the use of satire and parody, much of which is to be found, of course, in the closely-related Irish literature.

There is not the space in this book to examine in any detail these forms of cultural expression, or indeed such aspects as the school of stone-carving which flourished in Argyll. The agriculture practised by the population of the Highlands and Islands, their styles of building and their 'folk' ways are equally outside the scope of these pages, but have received expert consideration elsewhere. What is far more elusive is the question of what a clan was like. That they all spoke Gaelic and perhaps wore a district tartan can be agreed; that they were all related is not the least bit surprising in a land of sharply defined geographical units and in an age when travel was not much indulged in. The most vexed question, and one that becomes crucial later, is that of the relationship between the chief and the clan. Most people know that clan means 'children' and recent social trends may be obscuring the authority of the chief implicit in the word. That there were mutual responsibilities between chief and clansman is clear, and there also seems little doubt that there did genuinely exist close links between the various levels of society within the clan. The custom of fosterage, by which a child of the chief was placed in the care of a clansman and so brought up, is well documented, and must have done much to weave the various social strata together.

It is now quite often suggested that this close society got by entirely without the use of formal documents and, in particular, that the ownership of land was both informal and in common. Nothing could be further from the truth. There survives a number of the formal charters by which Highland chieftains held their land of the king. Even John of the Isles held land by charter of David II and his father Robert I. As the Lords of the Isles are now so often depicted not only as the 'Headship of the Gael' but sometimes also as the guardians of the true Celtic traditions, it is surely instructive to note that far from despising charters, there remain no fewer than 129 documents (either the whole text or fragments) issued by them; the bulk are in Latin, with four in Scots and only one in Gaelic. Many of these documents concern grants of land and such grants are to named individuals. The land-based taxation which seems to have originated with the Norse certainly continued throughout the succeeding period and this fact, in conjunction with the undoubted existence of these charters, does seem to indicate a more formalised society than many of its protagonists would admit. Whether the tenants of these feudal land-holders had any security greater than that of their counterparts elsewhere, or whether they could, perhaps by prolonged occupation of their lands, achieve such security, is far more difficult to decide. This is a question which will be seen to be of crucial importance later in this book.

Another aspect of clan life which is not easy to estimate is the extent of feuding – cattle raiding and so on – between the clans, as recounted in the occasional horror stories of whole populations being burned alive in churches or smoked to death in caves. Part of the revulsion that these stories may generate in the hearer must often result from ignorance of contemporary conditions elsewhere. Elizabethan England, for instance, was not a period devoid of social upheaval or of violence. The Highlanders were naturally martial, a surviving heroic society, if you wish, but the usual cause of their feuding was more prosaic – a lack of fertile land. This, allied to a growing population and the custom of primogeniture which gradually came to prevail, meant that there was always a lack of provision for younger sons, many of whom must have at times felt a need to supplement their incomes in much the same way as the Vikings had.

The Highlanders' habit of raiding the soft targets in the neighbouring Lowlands must have been the major cause of the hatred and scorn the Lowlanders traditionally maintained towards them. This is again an area where it is hard to get a clear picture; my own view is that this hatred did in fact exist; there are enough quotations extant from a later period to indicate that many prominent Lowland Scots felt that the Highlanders were an inferior and barbarous race. In view of the comment attributed to one Cameron of Lochiel regarding 'Murrayland, where all men take their prey', suggesting that places like Moray were deemed legitimate targets, this hatred does not seem completely unreasonable to me!

Things only got worse when individual kings of Scots decided to get involved north of the Highland line. Attempts were made from the time of James I to James VI to secure effective working of national laws in the Highlands and Islands, and to collect taxes. Lacking the resources which would be required for the effective, permanent control of such a large and diverse area, successive kings opted to police the Highlands through the promotion of one clan or another – both Clan Gordon and Clan Campbell, holding sway over vast territories, were used in this way. One inevitable result of such a policy was to deepen old divisions.

When religion was involved things only got worse, much worse. The National Wars of Religion (especially from 1643) and the Solemn League and Covenant, produced Protestant, Episcopalian and Catholic clans, encouraged old and new enmities and toppled kings (Charles I and James VII & II). The litany of dismal events which began during this period is all too well known:

1603 – Proscription of the MacGregors
1689 – Battle of Killiecrankie
1692 – Massacre of Glencoe
1715 – First Jacobite Rising
1719 – Second Jacobite Rising
1745 – Third Jacobite Rising
1746 – Battle of Culloden
1746 – Act of Attainder
1746 – Vesting Act
1746 – Heritable Jurisdictions Act
1747 – Disarming Act

The Risings themselves, especially the '45 with its tragic aftermath, are wrapped in so much romance that they are often completely misunderstood. It was not a case of Scotland versus England, or of Highland versus Lowland. Far from being simple and clear cut, they were messy affairs, civil wars with strong religious overtones. Some clans came in on the straightforward grounds of old loyalties or religious ties, but many must have struggled with thoughts of the political and military realities, or even the question of neighbourly advantage. In the end, those realities produced what was probably an inevitable result – having lost no battles, the Jacobite army advanced into England before realising that they simply could not hold the country through which they passed. So they retreated to Scotland and finally chose (for the first time under the orders of Bonnie Prince Charlie himself), the fatal battleground of Culloden.

Charles' own cousin, William Augustus, Duke of Cumberland, whom he faced across that battlefield, earned well his sobriquet of 'The Butcher' during the course of the subsequent vicious retaliation which he inflicted on the lands of the Jacobite clans. Charles escaped romantically into history and less romantically, but perhaps understandably, into a frustrated and drunken middle-age. The Highlands escaped nothing. The Acts which followed Culloden were designed to break the power of the chiefs and the spirit of the clansmen; they transformed what had been in essence a military and tribal society into a modern, money-based economy. The measures which achieved this are well known and included the notorious 'diskilting Act' (it was actually part of the Disarming Act) which was not repealed until 1782 (by which time it seems that Highland dress was once again widely worn). Sadly, for the Highlands, all this coincided with a period when throughout the rest of Britain traditional agriculture was being completely overhauled. The Enclosures of England are perhaps now less remembered than the Clearances of the Highlands, but at the time they caused only slightly less bitterness. Once they were completed, it was inevitable that the 'Improvers' would look northwards.

What they saw there, to them at least, offered all too much scope. After 1756 the raising of the Highland regiments to fight (somewhat ironically, it might be thought) for Britain during the Seven Years' War (1756–63) in America removed several thousand able-bodied men from all parts of the area. Many never returned. During this period of disruption and as a probable result of the diminished labour force combined with a long period of poor summers, the productive capacity of the land declined. This coincided unhappily with an undoubted desire on the part of the chiefs and tacksmen (their principal tenants) for a higher rental income, leading to greater poverty and voluntary emigration overseas. Several poor seasons led to near abandonment of traditional crops in favour of a growing reliance on the potato. Ultimately this had disastrous consequences when that crop failed in the famine of the 1840s.

These unhappy trends are generally understood to have been accompanied by a steadily rising regional population. This may be at least in part attributed to the productivity of the potato in the years before the blight, and in many coastal areas to the desire of the landowners to maintain a high population to engage in the profitable kelp trade. This – the gathering of seaweed for export to the south where its important chemical constituents were extracted – was a remarkably labour-intensive business, but prices crashed in 1815 when easy access to the resources of the Continent was restored. The Napoleonic wars, too, had ensured heavy demand for the black cattle which were the traditional mainstay of the Highland economy, but this, in turn, ebbed away after 1815.

In the meantime, the fashion for agricultural improvement had almost become a mania in Scotland. Just as it had been in England, the process of Enclosure was experienced, initially in the Borders and the Lowlands, and was at first bitterly resented. Evictions occurred in Galloway in 1723–4, in Wigtownshire, in East and Mid Lothian by 1730. A scientific approach to agriculture was adopted in many quarters with legal and financial changes made to facilitate the introductions of 'improving leases'. By the time innovative arable and stock farming had spread to Aberdeenshire and the

Laigh of Moray, it appears that enough of the indigenous population experienced real benefits from the improvements for them to be generally accepted, despite the inevitable and considerable disruption.

The process also began early in the Highlands and Islands, particularly in Argyll. Daniel Campbell of Shawfield bought Islay in 1725 and transformed its economy. Islay is, however, an intrinsically fertile island, which lent itself well to farming on the Lowland model. Much of the Highlands and Islands obviously required a solution of a different kind and sheep appeared to provide the answer.

There had always been some sheep in the Highlands, but the economy had traditionally been based on cattle. The decline of the cattle trade roughly coincided with the demands of the new manufacturing industries for wool, and experiments in cross-breeding had resulted in the creation of what appeared to be the ideal animal for the north – the Cheviot sheep. It was sturdy, highly productive of wool and meat, and appeared oblivious to the harsh climate of its native hills. The breed was introduced to Glengarry by 1782 and to Caithness ten years later by Sir John Sinclair of Ulbster.

The success of Sir John's sheep rearing venture at Langwell was clear and had wide repercussions. Imitators were numerous, but while plenty of landowners were happy to follow his example in introducing sheep to the glens, few, it appeared, were prepared to listen to his advice on its implementation. It was his view that tenants should, in essence, form sheep-rearing co-operatives and purchase small flocks, for which they would hire shepherds, paying rent partly in kind. Most landowners preferred to secure for themselves the considerable profits that they could see deriving from sheep and the small tenants on the land were literally in the way. They would have to go . . . and go they did.

Kildermorie was cleared in 1792 (afterwards known as the Year of the Sheep); Farr and Lairg in 1807; and Dornoch, Rogart, Loth, Clyne, Golspie and Assynt between 1810 and 1812. It was the turn of Kildonan in 1813 and, notoriously, of Strathnaver in 1814. The process of Clearance was therefore well established and had received the backing of the law by the time it was the turn of Glencalvie. The New Statistical Account of 1840 records that William Robertson of Kindeace owned Greenyards and Glencalvie, which were together valued at 108 pounds Scots. It is mentioned that there were now large numbers of sheep – 30,000 fleeces being shorn in the Parish of Kincardine annually, 'but the system of turning whole straths, where formerly peaceful cottages were to be seen, into sheepwalks is becoming too prevalent'. At last, public concern began to be aroused. When, in 1844 William Robertson died, his son decided to attempt where his father had at first failed – foiled (as was so often the case) by the determination of the Glencalvie women – and writs of removal were once again handed out, this time to the men, who accepted them and consented to remove the following spring. By the time they did so, the Clearances had become a major issue nationally and *The Times* of London decided to send a 'Special Commissioner' to examine the story. His second report to the paper is often quoted and cannot here be repeated in full; a few lines will suffice to make its tone clear:

> Were any such clearances attempted in England I leave you to conceive the excitement which it would be certain to create – the mob procession, the effigy burning, and the window smashing with which every instigator and instrument in so heartless a scene would be reminded that there are principles of action which are thought more honourable, more worthy, and which makes living amongst our fellows more pleasant, than mere money grubbing.
>
> These poor Highlanders, however, apart from their naturally mild and passive nature, have been so broken in spirit by many such scenes, that not a murmur, not a remonstrance, escaped them in the completion of this heartless ejectment.

That this was an effective piece of journalism cannot be doubted; there is also no doubt that the emotional nature of the occasion led the writer to stray a little bit beyond the facts on occasion. His last sentence, addressed to the Editor of *The Times* reads: 'This unsought, spontaneous and grateful expression of feeling to you for being their friend is what their natural protector – their chieftain – never saw, and what his factor need never hope for.' Here we see that the cloak of romanticism was already enveloping the Highlands – Robertson of Kindeace had acquired Glencalvie by normal purchase and could in no way be described as the chieftain of the people of Glencalvie. Note also what an amazing transformation has occurred in the depiction of the Highlanders: the once feared, bare-buttocked savages, who only a century before had been mocked, stripped, raped, hung or shot in the aftermath of Culloden, were now 'naturally mild and passive'. To which one might be tempted to add one word: bitter. While such generalisations are always to be accepted with caution, the procession of events which this chapter has of necessity treated with shocking brevity, has unleashed whole libraries of books, by far the majority of which make such a transformation all too comprehensible.

That the Clearances remain such an emotive issue is hardly surprising. They are not far removed from us in time; the last occurred less than 150 years ago. That means quite simply that it is possible for people living now to have spoken, as I have done, to people who knew in their youth people who had been evicted. That there was hardship and misery seems indisputable; the despair of those who find that they have no choice but to emigrate (in an era when many of them would expect to end their days where they were born) seems quite understandable. The walker in the hills still easily finds the ruined, silent villages from which they were removed: the souterrain I looked at that day (*see* chapter 5) lies below one such village, and the cottage of my childhood (*see* page 15) was the shepherd's house, the one dwelling that succeeded that whole community. Are the romantics among us the only people who are touched by the pathos of such places?

Much debated is the question of right: we have seen that, contrary to popular opinion, the chiefs held their lands by charter, and therefore presumably did have the right to sell their property:

legally at least the land did not belong to the whole clan. But the idea that the tenants did gain some inalienable right to security of tenure, through long occupation, is not so easy to dispose of. There are references to people who had the status of 'kindly tenants', and it seems clear that some did acquire a sort of hereditary right, after being in possession for a stipulated length of time. The Napier Commission, set up at last to investigate the whole issue, put it like this in 1884: 'The opinion was often expressed before us that the small tenantry of the Highlands have an inherited inalienable title to security of tenure in their possessions while rent and service are duly rendered – an impression indigenous to the country though it has never been sanctioned by legal recognition'. The Napier Commission was largely composed of landowners, who might have been expected to adopt a sceptical attitude towards such claims, but they finally proposed a compromise solution which owes much to the idea of the kindly tenancy: the Crofting Acts of 1886 gave to the individual tenant security of tenure on payment of rent to the landlord, which must be some sort of vindication of the claims of the dispossessed.

That solution came too late for thousands, now scattered across the globe. They took with them much of the folklore and custom, music and dance, of their native land, arguably much of its vitality. The dislocation and upheaval inevitable in such a process, severing people from their land and its traditional management, led to the abandonment of such sustainable practices as coppicing, while the few shepherds who replaced the native population could not maintain their field walls and ditches, and worked much smaller areas of land, so that progressively it lost its fertility. Initially, it seems that some areas were grossly overstocked with sheep; the intensity of the grazing may have halted the regeneration of some of the native woodland, and in conjunction with heavy burning may have hastened the formation of the peat-hags of the higher ground. The inexorable march of the rushes and bracken began; the face of the Highlands was being changed for ever.

13: Orkney

ROUSAY

Rousay is one of the most Highland parts of Orkney, hillier than most of the other islands, and with more heather than all except Hoy. Its resemblance to the Highlands goes deeper; Rousay was the only island in the archipelago to suffer Clearances. While others, such as Shapinsay, were being laid out anew – new roads, field walls and houses being constructed and the population being resettled – the north and west of Rousay was being cleared of its human population to make way for sheep. The landlord who completed this task built for his wife a gaunt Victorian house which would do credit to any rainswept Highland glen.

This house and its neighbouring plantation, largely of sycamore trees, is dominant above the pier as you approach the island from Mainland Orkney. We used to arrive sitting higgledy-piggledy on the deck of the *Shalder*, mixed up with the groceries for the shop and the booze for the hotel, while Mansie, the skipper, chatted his way around the boat. Now a smart, landing craft-type ferry takes cars, minibuses, vans and far more passengers than before, past Wyre to the Brinyan pier. It is far more convenient, of course, even if it has far less atmosphere, but at least when last I travelled that way, the ferry was skippered and crewed by members of Mansie's family.

On a misty August morning, we were met and transported along the island's circular, single-track road, watching the jigsaw of island and water endlessly change as we drove around. Passing

Wasbister and the emptiness of Quandale, where once there lived a flourishing community, we were dropped above Midhowe.

The mist was lifting, the sun coming out, but the grass was still wet as we made our way down the steep hill, through the large, rectangular Victorian fields to the shore. As we descended, we were looking directly over the narrows to Eynhallow, the Holy Island, with the smooth shapes of the green Mainland fields beyond, stretching from Gurness to Costa Head. From Eynhallow and its reefs, there wafted over to us that haunting sound, the 'melodious moaning' of the seals that haunt the shallow waters. Just by the shore is a large hangar-like structure, and we made our way into its gloomy interior. Despite being enveloped in this relatively modern construction, the ancient tomb that is contained therein is hugely impressive; truly a great stone 'ship of death', the long chamber within the enormous mound being divided into sections or stalls by upright slabs. Here were buried, perhaps, the leaders of this farming community of 5,500 years ago.

Only a hundred yards or so away, and 3,000 years younger than the tomb, are the remains of an imposing broch tower, an Iron Age stronghold with its bold doorway looking, very draughtily one would think, out to sea. Its interior was divided into two apartments (each with its own hearth, stone cooking pot and well) by an audacious erection of tall slabs, utilised just as they had been in the old tomb.

Having duly inspected both these monuments and marvelled at them, we stopped for lunch in the sun, on the shore between them, where an almost square indentation into the regular sandstone makes a perfect paddling pool. Here we sat, and munched our inevitable sandwiches, as the fulmars flew calmly and repeatedly past. Further along, hauled out on the rocks, were the inelegant, slug-like shapes of common seals. The inquisitive, dog-like faces of others looked at us from a few feet offshore. A lone tractor trundled along the empty hillside behind us, while the sun glinted from all the farms across the Sound.

As one walks this shore, it soon becomes obvious that this section of Rousay's coast is one great archaeological site;

'Midhowe' means the middle mound, and there were here, not one broch, but, amazingly, three. Bits of one outcrop to the south of the tomb and erode into the sea – it is overlain by the abandoned houses, barns, byres and drying kilns of one of the fishing and farming communities, displaced from the island. Around the angle of a recent wall, across a small burn where watercress grows, the length of a short field takes you to an unmortared square structure which juts out from under a late field wall. Its masonry is superb, although some of the beautiful, regular stones are now falling out; it is probably some sort of tower, maybe Viking, attached to the gable-end of a hall, most of which is covered by soil that has moved down the steep field beyond the dyke. This fascinating and beautiful building just sits there, clambered over by everyone, unexplained, apparently unprotected from decay and ignored by archaeologists.

Immediately beyond is a long, narrow, roofless church, whose gables would collapse but for the buttresses which prop them up. It may lie over a much older building, possibly contemporary with the Viking tower – this later structure must have served the cleared community whose houses immediately adjoin it.

By this time, as you potter over the shingle and look for the bistort in the boggy patch, you are aware of the multi-layered nature of settlement in these favoured, fertile places. Every small bump in the grass appears likely to have significance – the next one is an unexcavated cairn, like Midhowe but smaller, the next apparently half a broch: what happened to the other half, you wonder, and then comes the probable answer – perhaps its stones were pinched for the construction of the Viking long-house that you may just be able to see in the summer nettles and dockens. Beyond, out on the low headland, a mess of rabbit holes, uneven turf and bits of black plastic indicates one of the most important Viking graveyards in the country.

By this time you may be getting bothered, not just by the sharp-billed, scratchy-voiced terns that dive at your unprotected skull. Is this really the way to leave a priceless part of our island, or our national, heritage?

hauled up their longships, and then hauled ourselves up the steep hill to the road. After regaining our breath, we continued a little way before stopping at the highest point to rest beside the road, have a cup of tea, and look out over the scene that surrounded us – interlocking shapes of green-gold land and light-flooded water; such an idyll of fertility that it was impossible for me to think of days when snow blanketed the land which seemed to cower at the foot of towering seas and immense wild skies.

From Westness, the single-track road potters on past small farms and attractive cottages, past fuchsia and hebe hedges and mimulus-lined ditches, and past more tombs, until once again the gaunt profile of Trumland House looms above its plantations as it looks across the narrow sound to the kindly isle of Wyre. This small island was home to the young Edwin Muir until his family were forced to move, part of the emigrations which, across the Highlands and Islands, went side-by-side with the Clearances, and drove families from the land.

Edwin Muir's family went to Glasgow, but he had spent fifteen years in Orkney, years which gave him vision, and helped make him one of our foremost poets. Several of his poems relate to his years in the Islands, and reveal a deep feeling for the land which his father had farmed.

This passion for the land unites the people who live North and West of the Great Glen. Whether it is the craggy croft-land of Assynt or the shining fields of Orkney through which we returned that evening, this feeling for the land pervades the area from end to end.

14: The Victorians and After

RECREATION, ROADS,
FORESTRY AND THE HYDRO

Possibly the cruellest irony of Highland history is that during the years when much of its population was being shipped overseas, the area began to become fashionable and to acquire all the trappings of romance and sentiment which have remained with it ever since. The sporting opportunities the Highlands offered – above all the chance to fish for salmon, shoot grouse and stalk the red deer – had been attracting rich southerners for many years when Queen Victoria and Prince Albert bought Balmoral Castle, and made the ownership of a Highland sporting estate all the rage.

It is worth emphasising that enormous sums of money were invested in these estates, which their owners probably only ever visited for three or four months in the year. At times it seems that every glen, no matter how remote (and several fairly out of the way islands such as Rum or Rousay) must have possessed its turreted, gabled, castellated lodge. A few were plain, some were quite preposterous, but between them all they do amount to a remarkable architectural heritage, which for obvious, if perhaps unworthy reasons, has not received the attention it truly deserves. Some were in fact very ugly: one of the later ones, Kinloch Castle in Rum – taking the prize as far as this writer is concerned – compensating by the ornate grandeur of its interior decoration and furnishings, which were, of course, all brought in by boat, like the stone for the building itself, which came all the way from Arran!

The lodges, imposing though they are, represent as far as investment was concerned – although their subsequent maintenance has often proved a real burden – only the tip of the iceberg: there were piers, roads, bridges, stables, home farms, game larders, laundries, lodge cottages, plantations, gardens, walks for the ladies, and so on. One of the finest legacies of the Victorian sporting estates is often the network of carefully built stalkers' paths which criss-cross the land; many of them survive in good state today and make a strong visual contrast with the crudely bulldozed tracks that have scratched across the landscape in more recent times. In some areas almost every loch has its dam and sluice for creating an artificial flood to encourage a run of salmon or sea trout. Money was spent on the Highlands as never before (or since?) and although it offered a source of stable employment to many, it brought with it an increasing polarisation of society, the results of which still remain. The habit of NOT asking the advice or opinion of local people, which still bedevils the whole area, got into full swing in this period; one small example of this practice was the location of the attractive estate village of Tomich in Strathglass, on the south side of its narrow glen, with the result that its houses never get the sun in the depth of winter, and can be bitterly cold.

The face of the countryside was much modified, in ways which, it is increasingly now being seen, may be seriously detrimental to the overall productivity of the land. There was increasing reliance on the planting of exotic conifers, and on the burning of the heather, either to provide the conditions which suited the desired heavy populations of grouse, or to provide an early bite for the sheep. In either case, regeneration of native trees may be suppressed, and bit by bit the underlying peat is charred and eroded away.

Ceaseless war was waged against predators of all kinds: falcons, eagles, foxes, wild cats, etc., were slaughtered in their hundreds. A few, like the osprey and red kite, were pushed to the point of extinction in Scotland, and are only now returning – of their own accord like the osprey, or being reintroduced like the kite. It is clear that our wildlife is never likely to regain its richness of only two hundred years ago.

If the wildlife was now being slaughtered, the remaining Highlanders, now tamed, were being visited and studied, even if they lived in places as remote as the daunting cliff-girt St Kilda. Folklore and legends were collected, songs taken down and translated (and sometimes mangled in the process), the music of the bagpipe was admired, and tartan spread everywhere – along floors, up walls, over chairs and sofas – there weren't enough tartans to go around, so new ones were invented, and still are!

The whole 'sporting estate' cult centred around the stalking of the red deer, and estates came to be valued by the number of stags they carried. This and the desire to improve the quality of the specimens that end up as heads on someone's wall – partly by culling of the weak and partly by winter feeding – has led to an enormous growth in deer numbers: they have more than doubled in the last forty years. While this has been happening, however, their range has been progressively reduced as large areas have disappeared under plantation. The stalking of hinds was never as prestigious as that of stags and, often, not as efficiently done. It is a peculiarity of red deer that the sexes live apart much of the year (except it seems where the population is small, as in Sleat), and the hinds occupy the heart of the territory. If their numbers expand, it is the stags who are pushed to the periphery and break out into areas where they were formerly not present (and are often not welcome) such as agricultural land. It has often struck me that the red deer is truly a victim of its own success; it is now, because of its numbers, simply regarded as a pest, but it is, of course, still a beautiful and interesting mammal.

Although it is hard to generalise for the whole of the Highlands and Islands, there is little doubt that this growth in the deer population cannot be sustained; a substantial cull is necessary to avoid further damage to the vegetation. Sheep are often maligned in almost every context in the Highlands – they can certainly, for instance, be a nuisance on the roads, but they have played an important role to date in helping to maintain the populations of the crofting areas, the often marginal lands to which those who were permitted to remain were pushed at the time of the Clearances. It has often been claimed in the past that sheep are simply inimical to the growth of trees, but the notable regeneration of birch that has, for instance, taken place in Assynt (where there are still quite a few sheep!) in the last thirty years, means that the matter cannot be as simple as that. Where sheep are certainly much less effective than cattle is in trampling down and cutting into the underground rhizomes of bracken – they eat around the tall shoots of this most pestilential plant, thereby eliminating any competition.

One thing may at least be said of the upper-class Victorians who came to the Highlands each year: they appreciated the magnificence of the scenery and the recreational opportunities afforded by this wonderful landscape, and cared little for the vagaries of the weather. Those attitudes are now shared by others, in far greater numbers: some come for the rather alien and competitive purpose of 'conquering' mountains (as if one ever could!) or 'Munro-bagging'; others to look at wildlife or to study rocks and plants, but there are still some who just come to wander and enjoy the challenge of open space that is so much in contrast to the bulk of our overpopulated island. Recreation and tourism are often decried and derided, but that very recreation helps some people to stay sane and gives meaning to their crowded lives.

Despite fluctuations, tourism has grown this century to be a major source of income in an area where at times there has seemed to be almost no other. For long enough, after the First World War had decimated the adult male population, the Highlands and Islands were regarded as a depressed area. Attempts to inject the lifeblood of industry into its weakly pulsating arteries had come and gone like the west-coast herring, but were given renewed impetus after the Second World War.

The first wave of modern development was effectively three-pronged: being based on road building, forestry, and hydro-electricity. All three industries were labour intensive and between them they effected a real transformation of vast areas of the Highlands. New villages, largely populated by those employed in

Sheltered western sea-lochs like Loch Eishort in Skye are rich environments, home to seals and otters

Deer numbers and climatic effects mean that there is little regeneration
of woodland towards the western end of Loch Affric

In a gorge created between two rock types, the sheltered, humid environment is carpeted with mosses and liverworts. Oak and wych elm growing here reflect the varied nature of the original woodland of this part of Skye. Flowers like sweet woodruff and sanicle can be found

Looking from the old rocks of Sleat, with scrub-oak growing on a crag, across a peninsula composed of younger sedimentary rock, to the dramatic Black Cuillin, which are volcanic in origin. The shallow, sandy inlet of the sea is a rich marine environment, well populated by seals

forestry or by the Hydro Board, were connected by new, double-tracked roads. Cannich in Strathglass is a good example of such a village, its hotel having been the home of the hydro construction workers. All the glens of the surrounding area, the catchment of the River Beauly, were transformed by hydro schemes; one of the lochs so created, Loch Beinn a'Mheadhoin, was sensitively handled and is now often regarded as one of the most beautiful in the Highlands. It is in some ways fortunate that it is surrounded by remnant Caledonian Pine Forest, which lends it great beauty. The sides of most of the other glens were cloaked in vast monocultural plantations – many in this one area were at least of Scots Pine, but old native trees were often ignored or given no opportunity to reproduce, being densely underplanted, frequently with exotic stock.

The road building effected enormous changes in mobility, as far as it extended, so that the journey from Inverness to Ullapool, which was apparently a test of nerves in the 1930s, could probably be justly rated as one of Britain's most enjoyable driving experiences in the late 1990s. Unfortunately, the programme never went quite far enough; it is not possible yet to drive from west coast to east in Sutherland, for instance, on a double-track road, and part of the so-called trunk 'Road to the Isles' – the notorious road to Mallaig – remains a nightmare. The culmination of this road building was, of course, the reconstruction of the A9, the major highway into the Highlands. This was little short of a transformation, and it is still a good road, but it is also one which proves the force of the adage that the volume of traffic will soon increase to fill the new road space available.

What the new A9 undoubtedly helped to do was to bring the Highlands, especially the rapidly-growing inner Moray Firth area – and the Speyside tourist resort of Aviemore – into easier reach of the main British centres of population. The development of the oil industry which was to transform Shetland and to benefit Orkney significantly, put real impetus behind the growth of the inner Moray Firth, which had got rather shakily underway on the inappropriate basis of an aluminium smelter (now defunct) at

Invergordon, unhappily located on some of the finest agricultural land in the country.

Perhaps at first despite, but latterly certainly with, the aid of the Highlands and Islands Development Board – now Highlands and Islands Enterprise – few parts of the whole area have not seen great changes in the last thirty or forty years. In many places, after decades of decline, the population is at last rising, new schools have been built and confidence is growing. There have been many facets of this development; while it may be invidious to single out one above all others, it seems to the present writer at least that it is the rise of fish-farming which has done the most to stabilise the populations of the truly rural areas. Nearly every sea-loch on the west coast seems to have its cages, and where there are cages, men are employed to tend them. Like any industry, it has its problems, but we must hope that they remain problems with which it can cope, as much rides on it.

15: Skye

MINGINISH

The day dawned gloriously, promising to be hot – yet again! – what an amazing summer this had proved to be. I was up early, but even as I drove along the rough switchback road from Aird, the tar was already beginning to melt – through the open windows of the car I could hear it sticking to the tyres. Sleat is beautiful, well-wooded along the roadside, with views across the Sound to Knoydart, remote and depopulated, sometimes bleak and forbidding even at a distance, but now serene in the sunshine. Serenity was, however, not always my mood on this lovely summer morning; I was going one way along the single-track road that runs the length of the well-populated peninsula, and several large coaches were coming the other, no doubt heading for Armadale and the ferry to Mallaig. Some of the drivers blatantly took full advantage of the size of their vehicles, sweeping imperiously down the road and stopping for no one. In addition, there were many cars, motorbikes and cycles, and I spent much of the time diving for cover into passing places. The present road as it passes through the attractive crofting townships on this sheltered east coast of Sleat, through its banks of bushes and wildflowers, is simply not adequate for the traffic which at peak times it now has to take, and the frustration that it causes to local users in the summer is entirely understandable. But how to devise a new road which will be able to accommodate this much increased traffic, without destroying the very character of this special place?

So I pondered, in between bouts of swearing, as I headed for Broadford and the double-track road. Broadford was full of people (and of vehicles), and their evident happiness and colourful attire gave the place a glamour that it does not always possess (despite its superb situation, looking to Raasay and Applecross).

The good road northwards, towards the heart of the island, was much easier driving, and I could appreciate the flowery verges and the wonderful background of mountain and island. The traffic was moving quite fast, and one was whisked past these desirable aspects at a speed which reduced their impact – this suited me, as I wanted to get to my destination and out of the car, but at the same time it was ushering other folk out of Skye – how does one resolve these varying requirements of transport in beautiful places?

We swept inland towards the great hills, over the divide between Loch Ainort and Sconser, and along Loch Sligachan to the hotel of that name, which is almost the very heart of Skye – certainly from here is seen one of its most famous views, that of Glen Sligachan overlooked by the hills – Glamaig, Marsco, a glimpse of Blaven and that splendid group of the Black Cuillin dominated by Sgurr na Gillean. I took the road west, through the smooth sweep of Glen Drynoch to the head of Loch Harport – this corner of Skye shows very clearly the corduroy-like imprint on the landscape of great areas of lazybeds. These are ridges of made earth, created by the labour of bringing in manure and seaweed from the shore in order to supplement a thin and meagre soil. In places they run incredibly high and steeply up the glen sides, and the labour which it must have taken to create them, in order to raise crops where otherwise none would grow, is simply staggering (why call them 'lazy'-beds?). They abound in Skye and are, of themselves, difficult to date. In places they may pre-date the Clearances and indicate the reality of the increasing population which was a factor in the lead up to those unhappy events. In other places, it seems that they result from the hardship that so often occurred when populations were evicted from inland glens to the coast where there was frequently quite inadequate land. In any case, once you have grasped, if you really can, the incredible labour involved, it is hard to pass such areas without a whole complex of emotions being evoked – sadness, humility, guilt that we have life so much easier . . . and some measure of gratitude that we have.

From here I turned towards Glen Brittle, heading once again towards the Cuillins – the road once more single-tracked, but this time I was at least going with the flow! The mountains here dominate the view, but in places the foreground is occupied by some rather dismal and ineptly located coniferous plantations. With a view, one trusts, towards improving at least ultimately their appearance, blocks of these are now being clearfelled, presumably to be replanted, but this only adds patches of present devastation to the overall effect. The plantation of conifers is probably the least reversible form of land-use that we have, so such areas, however inappropriate their original location here may now be felt, will always remain under trees – the only possible way of softening the effects of such past mistakes is to plant a really significant proportion of broadleaves – preferably those that are found locally.

I trundled down the glen towards the bay with its busy campsite by the sea. There is a large car park here, and a number of fit-looking individuals were kitting up and heading for the big hills – many dangled ropes and bits of climbing ironmongery, clearly about to spend the day in death-defying manoeuvres from pinnacle to pinnacle. Having all too obviously no such equipment or ambition, and feeling therefore rather inadequate, I slunk off (if one can slink hurriedly!) in the other direction. A dipper flew upstream just as I approached the swaying bridge which crossed the shallow river.

My way took me uphill at a steady gradient on to the high plateau of an apparently un-named and unfrequented western peninsula. I had views of the peaks of Rum and the lower headlands of Canna while out to the west were the Uists and Barra. It was really hot, but there was a faint movement of air from the sea which kept it bearable, and I was not overburdened with clothes; it is rare in the Highlands and Islands to have absolute confidence that the whole day will be brilliant, but today was just such a day and I took full advantage of it, carrying more liquid to drink than spare jumpers. I walked steadily on, now on the level of a layer of ancient lava-flow, looking at the yachts that sailed the shining sea.

Once past two small lochs and round the headland, I was heading northwest; here on a broad grassy shelf above the sea there is a large and prominent archaeological site, a circular stony mound which despite several visits remains enigmatic to me. Beyond it one climbs to a small, naturally castellated eminence, with splendid views to the Cuillin and northwards to that great and also apparently nameless headland west of Dunvegan, on which sit the flat-topped Macleod's Tables.

Here a narrow defile cuts into the headland, eroded by a burn that makes its way steeply down to the sea. I descended gently into its gully, above the point where the burn falls dramatically, and paused to soak myself in a pool, though I could scarcely find one deep enough. Here on the steep gravelly sides of the gully, heather grows better than on the flatter, wetter moors, and there is meadowsweet and St John's wort.

Going steeply uphill from here, one arrives at a truly green, grassy area, where it is clear, a considerable number of rabbits live. There are low, roughly circular mounds in the grass which probably represent sheiling huts, this attractive area of sweet turf being exactly the sort of summer grazing which would have been taken full advantage of, in the heyday of the Clans. In an age before fences, it was both useful and efficient to drive the animals up into the hills in the summer to utilise the flush of summer grass. Those who tended them slept in small, rough huts, which often contained cells where the milk, butter and cheese were stored. This particular sheiling is extensive and reaches to the edge of the high cliffs. I walked a safe distance in from its edge, and sat down for a while to admire the quiet, unhurried flypast of a rather tatty golden eagle, with several wing feathers missing.

Once it had disappeared, I continued on towards the north, following the cliff line as it slowly declined towards the entrance to Loch Eynort. It was easy walking, the sun was shining, the views were glorious; how could one not be happy on such a day? I was heading for, and ultimately reached, a small but quite imposing dun, set on a broad low stack of rock. Its sheer cliff had been an adequate defence around much of the circumference of the site and the wall appears to have been most substantial towards the landward side. I had a good look round, took some photos and then retraced my steps to the higher ground to the south. As I regained height, I noticed that there was some distance away from me, a sizeable herd of cattle of mixed colours – many black, some white, and others a brown that was really red. They looked beautiful as they grazed in the August sun along the tawny hillsides, against the amazing backdrop of the Cuillins – like something out of Irish myth, no wonder they were so prized by the ancient Celtic heroes, who lived in the dun by the shore. There were lapwing flying and calling beside them, too – still one of the best sounds of the Highland summer.

At this point, I passed close by a dark lochan set in a peaty level, and headed inland towards a couple of rather messy-looking hills; the name of one of them – Truagh Mheall – when translated seems to mean 'wretched lump', which is not exactly fair as I was to discover that it is a most wonderful viewpoint. I walked for a while beside the burn that comes down from below this hill, and looked at another probable sheiling site at its junction with another stream. That beautiful herd of cattle would once have been tended by lads and lasses spending the summer in these huts, looking across the Minch, day after glorious day. This may be dismissed as mere romanticising, a typical hangover from Victorian days, but if ever the Highlanders of old found joy in their lives and landscapes it must have been in the shielings and the summer.

I followed an old dyke up towards the 'wretched lump' and scrambled up its eroded sides to the flat summit, where I sat for ages, looking at the wonderful panorama of the Cuillin ridge, riven peak after riven peak. My binoculars showed me that it was a busy afternoon up there with the gods; every peak seemed to have its quota of tiny figures and I imagined that they would be queuing at critical points along the celebrated ridge, taking their turn to leap from rock to rock – you will gather that I am no rock-climber!

By contrast, my surroundings were empty, and with a great

sense of freedom and space, I descended to the shelf at the base of my unimportant hill, and swam happily in its small loch. Drying afterwards in the sun, I lay on the deergrass and dreamily surveyed the Small Isles of Eigg, Rum and Canna, and the whole glory of the west coast.

16: Waves of Change

THE REVIVAL OF GAELIC;
CROFTING & LAND REFORM

And so, quite quickly, the Highlands and Islands have changed. It is easy enough to see why fears have arisen from time to time that with change, with all the developments and improvements in communications and so on, something has equally been lost. Walking in Inverness's now pedestrianised High Street, one could almost be anywhere in Britain, and the same applies driving through the new suburbs around this fast-growing city – or equally driving through the surprisingly densely-populated west Mainland of Orkney, where many of the new houses owe nothing to the architecture of their predecessors.

There may be a useful analogy here with the evolution of language. For while it is a fact that the Orkney speech, for instance, has lost much of its individual vocabulary, it seems still to retain its distinctive accent (and the warm Orcadian character happily remains undiluted). And so it remains for so much of the Highlands and Islands whose people steadfastly refuse to become clones of the rest of the British population.

Language has been an important factor over much of the area. While Gaelic remained as a viable language of the community in the Outer Isles, elsewhere it long seemed to be in retreat, but now appears to be making something of a comeback. This is certainly so in Skye, particularly in Sleat where Sabhal Mor Ostaig, the Gaelic college, is based. Bilingual road signs, although some people mutter about them, are at least a visual indication that you are now in a place where there is an alternative language. Probably few holiday makers, however, realise that they also mean that this is an area where rural development has been partly propelled by the promotion of a language. Indeed, twenty or so years ago, few professionals would have believed that Gaelic itself would become a development tool, but that is what has happened.

The teaching of the language required, obviously enough, Gaelic-speaking teachers; the teaching of business studies in that language required multi-skilled teachers and new textbooks. This led, in turn, to all sorts of publications, to media studies, to the need for Gaelic-speaking journalists and so on. Sleat, some thirty years ago, was a depressed-looking backwater, with crumbling remnants of Balmorality and the usual fears for the one remaining primary school and other vital pieces of social infrastructure. But now the peninsula is transformed, repopulated and prosperous, a showpiece of the Inner Hebrides. Where once, to my mind, Skye was a place where I could always be sure of hearing old people speaking Gaelic, Sleat is now a place where young people may well be heard speaking the language.

While that may be to a significant extent the result of the movement towards Gaelic-speaking playgroups and Gaelic-medium primary schools, both now quite widespread, some of it must have been due to the remarkable impact of one of the earliest, and unquestionably greatest, Gaelic rock-band – Runrig. This group revitalised Gaelic music, made it popular with the young and accessible to many who did not understand a single word!

There has, in fact, been a renaissance of Gaelic culture, especially its music and dance, much of which is returning from the lands (especially, it seems so often, from Cape Breton Island) to which emigrating Highlanders took it in the nineteenth century. Step-dancing, for example, which had disappeared in this, its native country, has been taken up with enthusiasm all over the Highlands, and so, of course, people are required to teach it. Just like Gaelic, the arts themselves have become instruments of job creation in the new Highlands and Islands.

One area of criticism sometimes expressed about these new jobs is that they are often not held by local people, and this certainly applies in another field which has been rather more controversial than the renaissance of the arts. The undoubted richness of the natural history of the area has resulted in large parts of it being designated for the purposes of nature conservation. It is an unfortunate fact that the old Nature Conservancy Council often presented such designation in terms of restriction rather than of opportunity. This ineptitude engendered ill-feeling, which unfortunately had not completely died away before a new wave of designations, emanating from the European Union, began once again to revive it. The attitude of the officials dealing with such matters is crucial, and sadly it appears too often that such officials do not understand the historical basis for the strong attachment of the individual to his or her land, and the resentment they feel in having yet another body place limitations on what they can do with it.

It is all too often forgotten that the 1886 Crofting Acts were a compromise, which gave to the landlord the title over the land (and the rent), but not the ability to use it, and to the crofter security in his occupation of the land (on payment of the rent), but not the title. Subsequent Acts made amendments, but did little to alter the fact that both landlord and crofter had reason to believe that it was their land, and each resented, it often seemed, the other's very existence. While some estates worked away quietly at establishing good relations with their local communities, others never quite managed it, and some became a byword for ineptitude or restriction. The appearance of speculators in land, often from overseas, fuelled the growing fire and gradually the subject of land reform was more widely aired – though not for much of Caithness, Orkney and Shetland where owner-occupation is more the norm.

It was the crofters in Assynt who achieved the historic breakthrough. The Assynt Estate, which had for many years been one of the more controversial ones, sold a large part of its ground in 1989, nearly all in crofting tenure, to a third party who turned out to be a foreign speculator. After a short time, this individual got into financial difficulties and decided to sell, intending to split the land into several lots by which it was hoped to maximise the selling price. The crofters determined to seize their opportunity to regulate their own destinies, mounted a well-planned and vigorous campaign to raise funds, and in 1992 achieved their goal.

Since then, the movement towards the establishment of Community Trusts has grown. The need for some alternative to the current situation where fragile communities have no protection at all from the whims of a proprietor (who may virtually never visit the property, like the famous Dr Green of Raasay) or the operations of the market, have been repeatedly highlighted by problems in places like Knoydart or Eigg, both now invigorated through community involvement.

Difficulties, of course, show no signs of going away, and although on the one hand the European Union may provide funds for much-needed rural projects, on the other it adds to the problems in a very real way. The future of agriculture, and to an even greater extent that of fishing, appears from the outside at least entirely a matter of European politics, and very hard to influence if you live in Lewis or Rousay. And yet, the land and the sea are our most basic and immediate resources; their utilisation must provide the best hope for the maintenance of a viable working population into the future. Decisions about that land and that sea are now taken far away from the people they influence, the people who depend on those resources for a livelihood.

Access to resources will always be a burning issue in the Highlands. Some years ago, the writer was particularly struck by the position of Cannich, in the deep, sheltered, fault-guided Strathglass. Cannich is land-locked, well inland, surrounded by natural resources. The big rivers develop significant amounts of hydro-power, but none of it is owned or controlled by the community, and there remains hardly anyone who is locally employed in that industry. Likewise, the community does not own the great expanses of forest which surround it, and there is currently little fixed employment in this industry. A couple of hotels have access to river and loch, but the community owns or controls none of the fishing for the salmon which pass through it. There are at least a few locally-owned farms, but otherwise what is so conspicuous about the village is its isolation from the resources which surround it. When I suggested that privatisation of the Forestry Commission, which was at that time being discussed, should only go ahead if ownership of the surrounding forests were put into the hands of the community, a local woman said that she did not believe that the community could cope with such a responsibility. It is good to be able to record that all over the Highlands, in Community Woodland Trusts, people are proving her wrong.

Of course, similar communities in Norway operate on precisely the lines I was suggesting. It is not our haphazard-looking geography, our unyielding geology or unrelenting climate that most effectively differentiate the Highlands and Islands from neighbouring Scandinavia (although there are some differences); it is our recent history which has so sundered our small communities from the resources that surround them, which makes the distinction so clearly. Redressing that imbalance will always be a real live cause in the Highlands and Islands, and for that reason alone, our communities will never be carbon copies of those elsewhere in the UK.

17: Skye

SLEAT

After a cold, wet and windy winter, when at times even the most devoted Northerner wonders why on earth he or she actually lives here, the first real spring day is one of almost overpowering magic. The signs of renewal have up until this day seemed so tentative and unconvincing, the first green leaves and shoots too tender to survive the next cold blast. Spring in the Highlands is the one season we often seem to do without; we can go to bed in early May with the rain, sleet or snow drumming on the roof, and the wind rattling the windows, convincing us that it is still winter – and awake to a transformed world.

So it was in Skye on 3 May 1995. When I awoke, what hit me first of all was that it was warm – genuinely warm – and I was sure that the soft mist was going to clear. I had spent the previous foul day doing accounts, and was determined to seize this day and devote it to something better!

I chose one of my favourite walks, one which did not entail much driving, and soon I was parking my car beside an old stone sheep fank under a steep quartzite hill. Even as I opened the door, I heard my first cuckoo of the year, and while I put on my walking boots, there were willow-warblers singing from every bush. Some of the young birches were just coming into leaf, that first tender, brilliant green that is so vibrant against the sombre tones of the winter hill.

I climbed steeply up through an oak wood (presumably planted, because of its complete lack of any other sort of tree) on the sunny side of the glen, and made my way along the hillside high above the new metal fank, heading roughly eastwards until the back of the high, shining quartzite ridge was to my left. At this point, I went north over the boggy saddle, from where I followed the headwaters of the burn which started to descend steeply, making for the waters of the sheltered sea-loch before me. I knew this way well, and remembered not to descend too early into the deep bed of the burn, having been trapped once or twice before by vertical waterfalls and steep rocks. Eventually I gingerly made the headlong descent into the narrow gorge.

This is a completely different world from that of the surrounding bare moorland. Except where it is too steep, the rather rotten rock of the gorge sides is clad with trees, and carpeted with mosses and liverworts. In high summer, the place is full of ferns, but these had hardly begun to shoot. There are fallen trees and collapsed branches everywhere, all furry with green-gold moss, and ivy and honeysuckle hang in crazy tangles off the cliffs. There were woodland flowers in bloom, wood anemone and primroses, with the deep glossy leaves and one early flower of sanicle.

I happily pottered about in this magical, undisturbed place, looking at the flowers and trees. There are some oaks higher up the gorge sides, but the big old trees, multi-trunked and full of character, deep in the burn-bed, seem mostly to be wych elm. Having fought through a tangle of fallen limbs, I followed the burn through easier ground, down to the sea and, stopping just a little above it, sat down to have my lunch in a place with a good view of the upper part of the loch.

I sat at the edge of the birches, munching my sandwiches and listening to the woodland birds around – great tits, willow warblers, wrens, chaffinches and a distant cuckoo, and then calling loudly and clearly, two other birds headed for me. I got an excellent view of them both, which made it all the more embarrassing (even on my own!) for me not to be able to make up my mind what they were. The choice was, I thought, between linnet and redpoll, but I just could not remember the distinguishing marks between them, where the splodges of red should be, nor a thing about the call of either bird, so in the end on the grounds of habitat alone, I opted for the redpoll.

The surface of the water, silk-smooth under hazy sunshine, was empty of birds – save one, and it was with relief that I recognised the familiar profile of a wintering great northern diver. (They always seem to hang around until you are sure that they must be going to stay and breed, then they disappear!)

Leaving the trees which follow the line of limestone parallel to the high quartzite ridge, I walked slowly along the increasingly rough shore to a point where a small rocky promontory juts out into the loch. There is a little bay to its east, where a boat could easily be hauled ashore, and the site has excellent views up to the head of the loch and out to the open sea. Landward of the little rocky headland, there is an area of flatter land, and discernible in the winter amongst all the dry, scratchy bracken stalks (and, sad to say, pieces of blown plastic) there are the foundations of what I would really like to be a Norse longhouse – it is just the sort of site they should have occupied! (But I have in all honesty to admit that it is hard to make out any real shape in all the vague heaps of stone.) I continued for a while, to a small sand beach at the mouth of another burn, where I sat watching the loch. Here there were curlew, more great northerns, guillemots and tysties (black guillemots), and a couple of eider duck. I have always loved the spring, woodwind-like call of the eider, and today for only the second time that I can remember, I heard in the hazy distance that wonderful combination of musical sounds: the mingled calls of eider and cuckoo.

I daydreamed for a while, then pottered about on the beach, looking for shells. I even ventured into the sea, but it was bitterly cold to my bare feet, and I had to be content to walk along its edge, where the smooth ripples lifted the coral sand like dust. The view to the west and seawards was as glorious as you could find anywhere – the clear blue of the loch backed by the jagged, purple-blue heights of Blaven and the Cuillin, and to the southwest the distant peaks of Rum. As I watched, a small lobster or prawn boat appeared round the headland, making its way to the township and jetty much further up the loch, its wake cutting deep furrows into the smooth enamel of the water. The ten or so common seals on a rocky islet close to me, heard, watched, but made no move.

Eventually, I dragged myself away, following the Rough Burn into trees and limestone country. Here the young grass was a real green, obscured in places by the last rust-red of dead bracken, and I wandered happily along, among the sheep and tiny, bleating lambs. In this stretch of country there are a few amazing, vast, old hawthorns. One of them presumably once grew upwards as a normal bush, but has collapsed and split, since when each half has grown to a great size, sundered from the other by at least ten feet. Hawthorn seems positively to flourish on land that is old pasture, and the limestone must always have been attractive to farmers. There are several old walls in this area, and a bit further along, I stopped to look at a recently-excavated Iron Age farmhouse beside a little burn.

Daylight was just beginning to fade as I returned to the car; it seemed that the warblers redoubled their singing, and the crying of the lambs filled the soft, warm, hazy evening air. The year had turned from dark to light, the ongoing purpose of nature was working itself out, all was well with the world.

18: The Walk to Ardvar

MARCH 1996

I start the walk just in from the wide gate with its conifers – the trees were not there thirty-five years ago, nor was the park where I leave my car, nor the tarmac road I follow. It is quite wide, with a great, broad verge, and I lose all sense or memory of the narrow track we once used. On the right, as the road goes downhill, are the tumbled remains of what might be shieling huts, on the left some mossy old walls. The small birches I remember in the heather below the path have grown up, dense and white-stemmed. If a drive had not been cut for the electricity poles, the inmost reaches of the sea loch below would not be visible.

Its orange wrack, the grey stones of the dun (a broch, a Pictish fort, say the voices of my memory), the faint traces of the old, tumbled graveyard, and the big stone fank with its substantial shed, all seem unchanged. The grass of the field behind the fank is now beginning to go green, contrasting with the deep purple of the winter birch. A heavy, squally shower comes racing towards me from Meallard, beyond is the blue sea, waves running white against all the islands in Eddrachillis. I shelter behind a dyke as the hailstones briefly whirl, and when it has passed and the sun shines again, a redwing hops along the verge.

Past the imposing dyke (Victorian?) there is, all at once, a new house – someone has been working outside. Beyond are boats, sheds, tanks, the noise of things moving, of people working. Six cars are lined up in the park. All this is new, and a little strange. There are people around, but I am hand-in-hand with the ghosts of the past, black-skirted, tweed-clad, soft-voiced, and for once I am not so keen to be seen, not so happy to stop and talk.

There are oaks, which I do not remember, behind the car park, celandines in bloom at their feet, little golden suns, the first of the year. A buzzard flies from the trees, its underwing pale in the light, much patterned, and a pied wagtail bustles ahead.

At the end of the twisting road, is the lodge, transformed, doubled in size, with a garden and many new trees. The area where we had clipped the sheep, untidy with bits of fleece and droppings, is now ordered gravel, the old sheds where the woolsack was hanging, are now tidy garages. What has become of the blushing youth, I wonder; I find that I cannot remember his name, and that annoys me.

But as I stand there, looking out through the garden to Meallard where deer are grazing on the greens, there is nothing sad in all the changes that I see in this familiar place. The house is lived in all year round, when once it was but a holiday home. A boat goes past to the salmon cages which employ people where, for many years after the sheep were put off the land, there was no work. Beyond is that familiar, fascinating, intricate landscape of the Lewisian Gneiss, the oldest rock in the world and, towering over it, the splendid profile of Quinag, abode of my personal gods, mountain of my heart.

Through many changes, the Highlands and Islands and their people remain. Though some of us may never own an inch of this land, we have our sure place in it, and are lent something of its strength when we have need of it.

Envoi

Scant are the few green acres that I till,
but arched above them spreads the boundless sky,
ripening their crops; and round them lie
long miles of moorland hill.

Beyond the cliff-top glimmers in the sun
the far horizon's bright infinity;
and I can gaze across the sea
when my day's work is done.

The solitudes of land and sea assuage
my quenchless thirst for freedom unconfined;
with independent heart and mind
hold I my heritage.

ROBERT RENDALL

A Rough Chronological Framework

Approx dates	Characteristics	Sites (remarks)
c.8000 BC	**'Middle Stone-Age'** *hunter-gatherers*	?Inchnadamph; Assynt (doubtful)
c.6500 BC		Kinloch, Rum (small population, perhaps nomadic)
	cave sites	Ulva, Oban
	'ledge' site	Staffin, Skye
	shell-middens	Oronsay (Colonsay)
	tent-like structures?	Jura
c.4000 BC	**'New Stone-Age' farmers**	(climatic optimum)
c.3800 BC	*early houses*	Knap of Howar, Orkney
c.3500 BC	*early chambered tombs*	Midhowe, Rousay (tools only of stone, wood and bone)
c.3000 BC	*village houses*	Skara Brae, Orkney
	? temple	Stanydale, Shetland
	chambered tombs	Maes Howe, Orkney; Camster Cairns, Caithness; Rudh' an Dunain, Skye
c.2800 BC	*henges, stone circles*	Ring of Brodgar, Orkney; Callanish, Isle of Lewis
c.2000 BC	**'Bronze-Age' farmers** *burials, sometimes cremations in stone cists set in earth mounds/ barrows*	(Bronze mainly for prestige use) Knowes of Trotty, Orkney
c.1600 BC	*(onset of climatic deterioration, restricted area of workable land)* *burnt mounds =? communal cooking sites* *early round-houses ('hut-circles')*	Liddle, Orkney and ubiquitous Lairg, Sutherland and ubiquitous
c.500 BC	**'Iron-Age' farmers/ Warrior Celts** *roundhouses* *brochs* *promontory forts* *hill-forts* *vitrified forts* *duns* *souterrains*	(outbreaks of conflict, use of iron weapons and tools) Ord, Sleat, Isle of Skye Mousa, Shetland; Glenelg, Inverness-shire; Dun Dornadilla, Sutherland; Dun Carloway, Isle of Lewis; Clachtoll, Assynt Ness of Burgi, Shetland; Rudh' an Dunain, Skye; Rudh' an Dunain, Assynt Ben Griam Beg, Sutherland; Craig Phadrig, Inverness Inverpolly, Wester Ross Ardvar, Assynt and ubiquitous Eriboll, Sutherland; Kirkwall, Orkney

A SIMPLE GEOLOGY

NOTE: All dates are very approximate. Rock-type names are generalised 'family names' and may no longer be used by geological experts.

From ~ (Years Ago)	West Highlands	Central Highlands	East Highlands
3,000m	*Lewisian Gneiss* Part of ancient earth's crust, complex and heavily meta-morphosed (Outer Hebrides, Assynt)		
1,000m	*Torridonian Sandstone* Massive sandstone, laid down in thick bands: forms near-vertical cliffs: largely impermeable (Coigach, Torridon)	*Moine Schists* Sedimentary rocks, folded and metamorphosed; impermeable (Central spine of Highlands)	
800m	*Cambrian Quartzite* Splintery, hard quartzite, caps peaks or forms dip-slopes; impermeable (Assynt, Torridon)		
500m	*Durness Limestone* Porous, forms caves, underground streams, etc. (Appears from Durness to Sleat)		